PENG
H

Anne Curry is Professor of Medieval History at the University of Southampton. Her books include *Agincourt: A New History* and (with Glenn Foard) *Bosworth 1485: A Battlefield Rediscovered*, and she has made numerous appearances on BBC radio and television. A former President of the Historical Association, Anne is chair of the Agincourt 600 Committee in conjunction with the Royal Armouries.

ANNE CURRY

Henry V
Playboy Prince to Warrior King

PENGUIN BOOKS

PENGUIN BOOKS

UK | USA | Canada | Ireland | Australia
India | New Zealand | South Africa

Penguin Books is part of the Penguin Random House group of companies
whose addresses can be found at global.penguinrandomhouse.com.

First published by Allen Lane 2015
First published in Penguin Books 2018
001

Set in 9.5/13.5 pt Sabon LT Std
Typeset by Jouve (UK), Milton Keynes
Printed and bound in Great Britain by Clays Ltd, Elcograf S.p.A

ISBN: 978-0-141-98743-9

www.greenpenguin.co.uk

Contents

Introduction

On 2 December 1420, the Chancellor of England, Thomas Langley, Bishop of Durham, addressed the assembled Lords and Commons at the opening of Parliament at Westminster. 'We people of England,' he began, 'have very special reason to honour and thank Almighty God.' The reason, as nobody present would have needed reminding, was the 'high grace, victory and achievement' that God had granted to England's king, Henry V. Langley enumerated these achievements: 'the suppression of the Welsh rebellion in his youth', and later, when king, 'the destruction of heresies and Lollardy within the kingdom'. But Henry V's crowning glory, sealed by the Treaty of Troyes some seven months before, on 21 May, was

> the recovery of ancient rights pertaining to his crown of England in France and in the blessed conclusion of peace and unity between him . . . and his former adversary of France . . . to the glorious pleasure of God and to the undoubted advantage and happiness of all this kingdom of England.[1]

At the eastern French city of Troyes, Charles VI of France had recognized Henry V of England as his rightful heir. By the treaty terms, on Charles's death Henry would become King of France – and in doing so he would turn the dream of English kings, ever since Edward III declared himself

King of France in 1340, into reality. In the meantime, Henry would be regent for the mentally and physically ailing Charles, whose daughter Catherine he married two weeks after the signing of the treaty, on 2 June. Once Henry succeeded his father-in-law, and for all time to come, the two thrones of England and France would be united under the same ruler. The treaty ordered an immediate end to all animosity between the two realms and their peoples, a remarkable outcome when the last two centuries had been dominated by war between England and France.

Then, the unexpected happened. On 31 August 1422, just twenty-one months after Langley's encomium to Parliament, Henry V, aged almost thirty-six, died from 'the bloody flux' at the great fortress of Vincennes, east of Paris. Predeceasing Charles by six weeks, he was the first English king to die overseas since Richard I over two centuries earlier. His nine-month-old son by Catherine, Henry VI, was recognized as King of France following Charles's death, but Henry VI would prove as ineffective as his father had been assertive: within thirty years the English had been removed from French soil, save for a toehold at Calais. Henry V's double monarchy had failed.

Even so, in the popular imagination, Henry V remains as much a success story today as when Bishop Langley addressed Parliament in 1420. Indeed, he is often considered destined for greatness from the moment he came to the throne on 21 March 1413. His victory at Agincourt on 25 October 1415, still one of the most iconic English victories against a foreign enemy, achieved in the face of allegedly overwhelming odds, is viewed as the consequence of his astute leadership and personal bravery. What's more, this view of Henry as a successful warrior-king, inspired and supported by God and beloved of his people, has been constant throughout history. It inspired two Latin prose lives of the king in the late 1430s. The first was the anonymous *Vita et Gesta Henrici Quinti* ('The Life and Deeds of Henry the Fifth'), commonly known as the Pseudo-Elmham since it was once thought, erroneously, to be the work of Thomas Elmham, a monk of St Augustine's Abbey, Canterbury, who wrote a verse account of the opening years of the reign. The Pseudo-Elmham appears to have drawn information from Sir (later Lord) Walter Hungerford, much trusted by Henry as councillor and commander, and chosen by the king as one of the executors of his will and guardians of his infant son. The second Latin life of the 1430s was Tito Livio Frulovisi's *Vita Henrici Quinti* ('The Life of Henry V'), written while the Italian was in the employment of Henry's youngest brother, Humphrey, Duke of Gloucester. This work was dedicated by its author to Henry VI in the hope that he might emulate his father. In 1513–14, a *First English Life of King Henry the Fifth* was written, drawing on Tito Livio's *Vita* and on collected reminiscences from the 4th Earl of Ormond (1392–1452), who had known Henry V, but dedicated this time to Henry VIII as a potentially worthy successor of his illustrious namesake.

The Tudor chronicler-historian Edward Hall echoed earlier positive portrayals in his *Union of the Two Illustre Families of Lancaster and York* (1542), applauding the 'victorious acts of Henry V' in a work which otherwise demonstrated how the 'unquiet time' of the usurper Henry IV

(1399–1413) had initiated a century of upheaval not resolved until the 'triumphant reign' of Henry VII. The great collaborative work known as *Holinshed's Chronicles* (1577, 1587), which was Shakespeare's main source, made extensive use of Hall's text. It is hardly surprising, therefore, that the same eulogistic tone was reflected in Shakespeare's *Henry V* (1599). The popularity of the play from the mid eighteenth century onwards, fanned by recurrent wars with France, and its stirring speeches (so memorable that even today some want to believe they are Henry's actual words) have made Henry V one of, if not the best-known and most admired of all medieval English kings. Even academics have succumbed: the great twentieth-century historian K. B. McFarlane, not known for his breathless admiration of monarchs, concluded that 'all round', Henry V 'was, I think, the greatest man that ever ruled England'.[2]

Yet Henry was not born to be king at all. His life was a series of transformations. His father Henry of Bolingbroke's usurpation of the English crown as Henry IV in 1399 transformed him from 'the young Lord Henry', a member of a collateral line of the English royal family, into the Prince of Wales. In his portrayal as heir to the throne, the popular image is again that of Shakespeare. Hal in *Henry IV, Parts 1 and 2* (1597–8) is all that a prince should not be – disrespectful, pleasure-seeking, indolent – but on becoming king at his father's death, he consciously casts aside his former life and friends and reveals himself transformed into the perfect king. The real Henry can also be shown to have changed fundamentally at his accession, at his own choosing, into an overtly religious, celibate and unbending ruler.

He sought to redeem his poor personal reputation and expiate his troubled relationship with his father. He also sought to rebuild his political and military standing at home and abroad.

The Agincourt campaign of 1415 was part of this process of conscious rebranding. It was also a point of transformation which set Henry on course for further achievements as a warrior-king. In 1420 these successes generated his final metamorphosis into the effective ruler of France. Yet this last achievement brought with it new problems of kingship in both England and France. Was it really feasible for one man to rule both kingdoms in this age of personal monarchy?

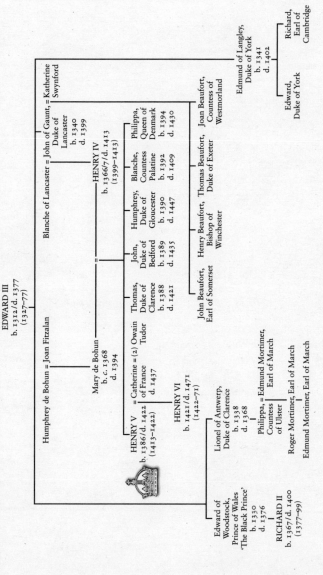

Henry V

I

From Young Lord Henry, to Prince, to Political Outcast

According to an astrological treatise written during his own reign, Henry V – or, as he was then known, 'the young Lord Henry' – came into the world at 11.22 a.m. on the morning of 16 September 1386, born in a tower above the gatehouse of Monmouth Castle in the Welsh marches.[1] Later historians, misreading a financial record, gave him a fictitious short-lived elder brother;[2] but there is no doubt that he was in fact the first child of six born to Henry 'Bolingbroke', Earl of Derby – who at that point can have had little idea of the path that would lead him to ascend the English throne as Henry IV, the first Lancastrian king – and his wife, Mary de Bohun, then some seventeen or eighteen years old.

Henry V's birthplace was owned by his grandfather, John of Gaunt, Duke of Lancaster, the third surviving son of King Edward III and a major political force in the reign of Richard II. Monmouth was among the many lands and castles which had come to Gaunt thanks to his marriage to Blanche, heiress of the great earldom, and subsequently duchy, of Lancaster. As Gaunt's first grandson, Henry was the heir presumptive to this great duchy, the largest and most valuable landholding in England other than that of the crown, with major holdings in Lancashire and the Midlands but tentacles in East Anglia, south Wales and the Welsh marches or borderlands. An inheritance from his maternal ancestors could also be expected: Henry's mother was co-heiress with her sister, Eleanor, of their father, Humphrey de Bohun, Earl of Hereford and Essex, and the expectation was that their inheritance would be divided between their families. This prompted Richard II's granting of the title Duke of Hereford to Bolingbroke, another title his eldest son would expect to inherit.

Ahead of young Lord Henry, then, was a path that would lead him to becoming one of England's highest-ranking noblemen. As a member of a collateral line of the royal family, it was likely that, at the age of majority – twenty-one – or at marriage, he would have been given a title and a landed endowment, even in advance of coming into his full inheritance of the duchies of Lancaster and Hereford. As a peer of the realm, he would have been summoned to Parliament and involved in national and local politics and governance; he would have served in royal armies and embassies and perhaps, following in his father's footsteps, participated in crusade.

What we can glean of Henry's childhood from the financial records of his father and grandfather reveals an upbringing commensurate with his future prospects. The earliest known is the purchase of baby clothing (a demi-gown) for him at the age of one.[3] As was customary, he spent the first five years of his life with his mother, but he also had a wet nurse, Joan Waryn, whom he remembered when he became king, giving her a generous annuity.[4] Like

4

all aristocratic families, Lord Henry and his relatives and servants moved frequently between their various houses and estates. During his early years, we find him with his maternal grandmother (Joan Fitzalan, Countess of Hereford) at her house at Bytham, Lincolnshire, as well as frequenting his paternal grandfather's castles at Leicester and Kenilworth, which came to be one of his favourite places: as king, he would return there often, even building a special retreat for himself in its grounds. Seven books of Latin grammar bound together were bought for him in London when he was eight years old, around the age at which his formal education would have begun.[5] These would have included standard texts for learning Latin, such as the *Distichs* of Dionysius Cato, which also gave moral guidance. Later evidence indicates that Henry had a good knowledge of Latin and was conversant in French. Indeed, he appears a relatively bookish king, although the story that he attended Queen's College, Oxford, in 1398 is apocryphal.

Other purchases of the 1390s reveal different aspects of a noble upbringing as he moved towards his teens: swords, saddles and armour, a chain for his greyhounds, and the assigning of a group of servants to his care and tutelage, which included Peter de Melbourne, a highly trusted life retainer of both Gaunt and his son.[6] Henry's membership of a collateral line of the royal family led to his early presence at matters of state. In August 1396, shortly before his tenth birthday, the purchase of saddles with silver-gilt fittings 'for the journey to Calais' reveals that he had crossed the Dover Strait to attend the marriage of England's king, Richard II, to Isabella, seven-year-old daughter of Charles VI of France, a union which was intended to cement a thirty-year truce with France and facilitate the negotiation of a full peace.[7] During the negotiations there had been mention of Henry marrying Isabella's younger sister Michelle, then still only a year old, another option being the daughter of the Duke of Brittany, also aged under five. Even if not an active participant in such discussions, we can assume that Henry was already aware of the issues of Anglo-French relations which were to loom so large in his adult life. A year later, he was exposed to national government: robes were provided for him and his eldest younger brother, Thomas, for the parliament at which their father was created Duke of Hereford on 29 September 1397. Whether or not Henry heard his father make in the parliament allegations of treason against Thomas Mowbray, Duke of Norfolk in response to Mowbray's warning that the king intended to destroy both Bolingbroke and himself, or whether he was present in Coventry in October 1398, when the resulting duel between Bolingbroke and Mowbray was due to take place, is not known. But he undoubtedly felt the effect of Richard II's decision to abort the duel and to send both men into exile: Mowbray for life and Henry's father for ten years.[8]

Equally disruptive for the now twelve-year-old Henry was the death four months later, on 3 or 4 February 1399, of his grandfather John of Gaunt. Richard II decided that the exiled Bolingbroke should not be allowed to seek his inheritance of the duchy of Lancaster until he had served the full term of his exile. This placed the boy in a potentially difficult position financially since he could no longer be supported by his father or grandfather. Yet the king was keen not to disparage the young man. Within three weeks of his grandfather's death, Richard had granted him £500 per annum from royal revenues, although he seems not to have come to court but remained in the care of Peter de Melbourne. In early May 1399, he was allocated further funds towards armour and equipment for the king's expedition to Ireland, which Richard had decided he should accompany and on which de Melbourne also served.[9] According to Jean Creton, a French observer who later wrote an account of the Irish expedition and of Richard's deposition later in the year, the king dubbed Henry a knight during the campaign just before an anticipated engagement with Irish rebels.

The campaign was Henry's first experience of warfare. Even if we do not know whether he actually participated in action, it was common for noble boys to be taken on campaigns once they were twelve. But did Richard have an ulterior motive in taking Henry to Ireland – holding him as a hostage to ensure his father's good behaviour as an exile? If this had been the king's intention, then the plan failed. Bolingbroke took the opportunity of Richard's absence in Ireland to return to England in late June, ostensibly in pursuit of his duchy of Lancaster inheritance but in effect to mount a challenge to the throne. Richard was forced to come back to England but before he did so, he ordered the young Henry to be imprisoned in Trim Castle, thirty miles to the north-west of Dublin. By the time Richard arrived home through Wales, Bolingbroke had taken control of much of eastern and central England, and managed by 9 August to reach Chester, previously a major centre of Richard's power, before the king. Richard had no choice but to agree to negotiations, which led to his surrender and being held prisoner. Around 20 August, Bolingbroke led him from Chester to London. By the end of September, Richard had been forced to abdicate and Bolingbroke had seized the throne. He had already ordered his eldest son to be brought back from Ireland. A shipmaster, Henry Dryhurst, was paid just over £13 for sailing from Chester to Dublin and back to collect him.[10]

The unusual circumstances of the usurpation, and the change to the young Henry's fortunes as a result, fascinated contemporary observers and triggered speculation on the conversations that might have taken place between himself and Richard in Ireland when the news of Bolingbroke's invasion broke. The English chronicler Thomas Walsingham (d. 1422), continuing the chronicling tradition of the Benedictine house of St Albans, imagined Richard asking Henry: 'why has your father done this to me ... I grieve for your person in that you will perhaps be deprived of your inheritance because of this unfortunate behaviour of your father'. Henry's reply, 'though he was but a boy, was not childish ... "Gracious king and lord I am truly much aggrieved at these rumours but it is obvious to your lordship, in my estimation, that I am innocent of my father's actions."'[11] This pro-Lancastrian tale improved in the telling, serving to emphasize both Richard's deposition and Henry V's greatness as preordained. In both of the Latin lives of Henry V of the 1430s, Richard was made to foretell the future glory of Henry. As expressed in the Pseudo-Elmham:

> we have heard that our own England is destined to give birth to a certain Prince Henry who will be ... of exceptional grandeur in his deeds, of rare and immense military prowess, with outstanding titles of fame, and who will shine with prosperity throughout the whole world ... we are of the infallible opinion that this very same Henry is that man.[12]

The thirteen-year-old Henry had played no active part in the deposition of Richard – but he was a beneficiary of it and his life was irrevocably changed by it. He was probably among those knighted by his father on the eve of the coronation (12 October 1399).[13] He certainly carried the sword of justice at the ceremony itself, symbolizing his significant place in the new dynasty. Two days later, on 15 October, his creation as Prince of Wales, Duke of Cornwall and Earl of Chester was approved by the Lords and Commons in Parliament, who also expressed their wish to accept him as rightful heir to the throne on his father's death. Henry IV, enthroned, 'placed a coronet on the head of Henry ... and placed a golden ring on his finger and put a golden staff into his hand and then kissed him'. Henry, the Prince of Wales, was then led to the seat 'ordained and assigned to him in Parliament by reason of the principality'.[14]

Because of his father's need to secure his dynasty in the wake of a usurpation, Henry is the first eldest son of an English monarch known to have had a formal investiture as Prince of Wales in Parliament, and ended up holding a wider range of titles than any previous heir to the English throne. On 23 October, he was made Duke of Aquitaine as a means of confirming the new dynasty's commitment to English interests in south-west France. On 10 November, he was also created Duke of Lancaster, his father having decided that as king he could not hold this title himself although he continued to retain direct control of the revenues of both duchies.

The young Henry had been transformed from a landless and potentially defenceless prisoner in Ireland into a royal prince with substantial territorial interests. Yet just as he benefited from the trappings of royalty he had acquired, so he shared in the vulnerability of the new regime. The first anti-Lancastrian plot came only weeks later, on 6 January 1400, and the most high-profile victim was the prince himself, who along with others in the royal household allegedly showed signs of an attempt to poison them. The new regime's response was uncompromising: the leading nobles involved in the plot were put to death and Richard II was murdered in the hope of curtailing any further threats.[15]

Before long, however, the king faced hostility from his erstwhile friends Henry Percy, Earl of Northumberland, and his son Sir Henry Percy (known as Hotspur for his valour), who had been key supporters of his usurpation in 1399. Disappointed that the king had not rewarded them adequately during the first few years of his reign, they rebelled, bringing Henry IV to battle at Shrewsbury in July 1403. Although Hotspur and his uncle Thomas Percy were killed, the Earl of Northumberland was subsequently pardoned, only to stir up northern risings in 1405 and 1408. Both ended in defeat, but these actions heightened Lancastrian fears. The 1405 rising prompted an excessive reaction of the king in ordering the execution of Archbishop Scrope of York for his support for the rebels. The rebellion of Owain Glyndŵr in Wales – which began in the autumn of 1400 as a personal dispute with his neighbour Reginald Grey but which soon escalated into a campaign for Welsh independence – also became linked to a threat to the Lancastrian right to the throne. In 1403 there emerged a plan to divide the realm between Glyndŵr, the Percys and the young Edmund Mortimer, Earl of March, the descendant of the second son of Edward III. Technically, this Mortimer line had a better claim to the throne than Henry IV, who was descended from the third son of Edward III. In time, Henry IV also began to suspect the loyalty of Edward, Duke of York, heir to the fourth son of Edward III.

There were further anxieties for the new dynasty. Henry IV's usurpation undermined, although it did not break, the 1396 truce with France. The French, ruled by an increasingly ill king, were too divided among themselves to drive out the English from their French lands. But there was none the less major insecurity in the Channel for English shipping in the face of officially condoned French piracy as well as open war in Gascony, the last area held by the English in south-west France. A much more serious military problem was the insurgency in Wales, which dragged on for many years. This insecurity, both internal and external, brought with it financial difficulties: as a self-made, usurping king, Henry IV's authority was weak in terms of persuading

Parliament to agree taxation, and in being able to choose how to spend his income.

These uncertain, conflict-ridden years were also those of Prince Henry's royal apprenticeship. It was a time of almost constant military mobilization – something which is especially significant given that Henry V would spend virtually his entire reign in active warfare; indeed, he knew no other way to rule. Henry, Prince of Wales had a longer military formation as heir to the throne than any monarch since Edward I. His knowledge of English military systems, his service in arms in Wales alongside several of those who were to accompany him to France later, and his appreciation of the importance of discipline as well as the tactical value of archers, all stemmed from the experience he gained during this period.

In the early years of his father's reign, the prince's personality and outlook remain indistinct, his actions informed by the circumstances of the new and fragile regime. His creation as Duke of Aquitaine in 1399 was made with a view to sending the teenage prince at the head of an army to this potentially problematic part of the English royal inheritance, but the parliament of 1399 urged his father to reconsider: 'the prince should not leave the realm at such a tender age until peace has been more securely established within the kingdom'.[16] Henry IV duly followed Parliament's advice. When, the following August, he invaded Scotland with a 13,000-strong army, Prince Henry received pay for a company of 17 men-at-arms and 99 archers but, again, probably stayed at home, having been appointed keeper of the realm in his father's absence.

Owain Glyndŵr's Welsh rebellion erupted in September 1400, as Henry IV was returning from his brief and inconclusive campaign in Scotland. The king duly headed for the Welsh border, where he was joined around the middle of the month by Prince Henry. On 16 September, perhaps deliberately choosing Prince Henry's birthday to make his announcement, Glyndŵr had declared himself Prince of Wales: it was, therefore, essential that the real prince be present to put down the rebellion. Yet, as on subsequent occasions, for the sake of preservation of the dynasty Henry IV did not take his son with him on his *chevauchée* or raid into Wales. Instead, the prince was sent to his earldom of Chester with power to pardon those Welsh rebels prepared to present themselves to him.[17] Here he spent an extended period in the company of Sir Henry Percy (Hotspur), who was so trusted by Henry IV early in his reign that he was appointed justiciar (chief officer) of Chester in October 1399: the king clearly regarded him as a suitable military mentor for the prince. The latter was with Hotspur at the siege of Conway in April 1401 after Welsh rebels had seized the town. In the following month, the prince continued his military tutelage at the siege with Sir Hugh Despenser, a seasoned military campaigner and Lancastrian loyalist who had been appointed the prince's governor in October 1399. It took six weeks for Conway to surrender to the prince, his first exposure to the challenges of siege warfare.

In 1401 and 1402, still in his mid-teens, Prince Henry was again in north Wales. He was learning all the time, and it was here that he encountered the problems of dealing with guerrilla warfare in mountainous terrain: his baggage train was attacked by the Welsh and his possessions carried off. Occasionally, his father counselled him in the practice of war, in one letter urging the prince to ensure the sound defence of the castle of Harlech on the grounds that it cost less to defend places than to recover them, advice he would take to heart in his own conquest of Normandy.[18] At the age of sixteen, he was given his first formal command as royal deputy in Wales with an army of 3,000 for the field as well as for garrisons.[19] He tried to run to ground the would-be prince, but Glyndŵr melted into the hills, and Henry contented himself with pillaging the pretender's lands at Glyndyfrdwy. Writing to his father about this failure, he expressed fears that his troops might desert: with cash running out, he had been forced to pawn his smaller jewels ('petits joyaulx') to pay them and to order his men to carry oats with them since fodder was in such short supply within Wales.[20]

The prince was soon to learn an even harder lesson of the uncertainty of loyalties – one which surely remained with him all his life – when the Percys turned against the king in 1403. Several of those who had been in the prince's intimate company in Chester and Wales now revealed themselves as enemies, bringing him and his father to battle in order to effect a regime change, maybe even to make Hotspur king. These included not only Hotspur himself but his uncle Thomas Percy, who had been appointed the prince's governor at the death of Despenser in late 1401, and who, in the words of one chronicler, 'slipped away from the prince's house in secret and with much of his treasure'.[21] In the following year, even the chamberlain of the prince's earldom of Chester defected to Glyndŵr.

The Battle of Shrewsbury on 21 July 1403 was a hard-won fight for the king's army and for the prince, who had been entrusted by his father with command of the vanguard. Edward III had given a similar command to his eldest son, the Black Prince, at the Battle of Crécy in 1346 when the latter was sixteen years old. For the two princes this was a major military blooding, but it also served to encourage loyalty, confidence and perseverance in the troops of the royal army. At Shrewsbury, both armies had large numbers of archers, using them to create an opening barrage to weaken their enemy's attack. While the larger royal army was able to predominate, the prince was wounded by an arrow in the face. He gained plaudits for his personal bravery, especially for encouraging his troops to fight on and for refusing to leave the field. We have a fascinating record of the medical procedure he subsequently underwent at Kenilworth Castle at the hands of his surgeon, John Bradmore, to remove the arrowhead, which had become lodged in the side of his face. Bradmore devised an instrument with a screw device that enabled him to grip the arrow and pull it free. The surgeon helpfully drew a sketch of his instrument as well as describing the method used to cauterize the wound during and after treatment.[22] Without Bradmore's intervention, blood poisoning could easily have ensued. It is likely that the wound left Henry with a scar, although this is never mentioned in any contemporary descriptions of him as prince or king.

Perhaps because of his injury, Prince Henry spent most of

his time in 1404 on the English side of the border, sending his senior captains on raids into Wales. These were not enough to prevent Glyndŵr's power reaching its height in 1405, aided by French troops who marched with him as far as the prince's base at Worcester, and also took the castle of Harlech. There, Glyndŵr held a parliament in which – with considerable hubris – he announced his intention to broker a peace between England and France that would include an acknowledgement of Welsh independence. Such insults triggered Henry IV's plans for a big push by two 3,000-strong armies, one from Hereford under his own command, the other from Chester under Prince Henry. This initiative was thwarted by the need to respond to the rebellion of Archbishop Scrope, although the prince did not play a personal role in its suppression.

In January 1406, the prince was appointed lieutenant for the whole of Wales. The king had intended to remain involved himself, but the hostile activities of the French in the Channel forced him to return to London and to accept that 'the prince with his retinue and the power of adjacent counties, in whose loyalty the king places his trust, is in force enough to chastise and subdue the rebels of Wales'.[23] At this point, the prince had 5,000 men under his command with three archers for every man-at-arms, a contrast with the one-to-one ratio often found in the late fourteenth century for overseas expeditions. This three-to-one ratio dominated English military organization until the 1440s, including all the expeditions and garrisons of Henry V's own reign. While it is tempting to believe that it was the prince's innovation, his father may have been behind it in reality.

Despite the prince's central role in the conflict of these years, Henry IV was slow to give him independence before reaching his majority at twenty-one. This was, partly, due to the prince's tender age, but it was, too, an effect of the Glyndŵr rebellion itself. So comprehensive was the uprising in Wales that by 1403 none of the prince's estate revenues in Wales or Flintshire could be collected because of the disruption: funds from the earldom of Chester had had to be diverted to cover the costs of the Welsh castles still under English control. As a result, the prince faced a large financial deficit, which inevitably impacted on his ability to act independently.

His father's involvement is also seen in the choice of officials; tried and trusted duchy of Lancaster men were placed in key posts across the prince's lands. The king had an influence over the grants of annuities too. Such a situation was to be expected while the prince was under age, but as he approached his majority he would wish to exploit his own patronage and to build up his own affinity. He began to do this from October 1407. Fifty-one new grants of annuities were made in the course of the following year, a marked contrast with an average of ten per annum over the previous six years.

By this point, Henry IV's health had been in noticeable decline for eighteen months. The exact nature of his illness remains uncertain but it involved a degenerative skin condition as well as debilitating attacks, perhaps in the form of strokes or epileptic fits. The symptoms would fit with a diagnosis of tertiary syphilis, creating a protracted decline over around eight years but interspersed with more severe bouts which undermined his capacity to give full attention to government. As the king's health deteriorated, the moment of the prince's succession loomed ever larger: he might become king at any point. As in similar situations across history, the effects on both father and son were marked.

In 1406, Henry IV experienced major criticisms from Parliament, whose records suggest hopes for a better future were already focused on Prince Henry. Early that April, the Speaker, on the Commons' behalf, petitioned the king to send a letter of thanks to his son, for his constant commitment to winning back Wales, 'and for the chastisement and punishment of the rebels there'; in the same address, he urged that the prince should 'reside continually in Wales for the wars'.[24]

Two months later, with Henry IV present in Parliament, the Speaker took the opportunity of making another eulogy on the prince. 'God had bestowed and endowed him with a good heart and as much courage as any worldly prince could need,' he stated, adding that God had given him 'one great virtue' in particular: he listened to his advisers. Indeed, such was the prince's trust in them that he was 'genuinely and graciously willing to be contradicted, and to conform to the wishes of his council and their ordinance, in accordance with whatever seemed best to them, setting aside entirely his own will'.[25] Not only did the prince listen, but advice could be plainly given, without fear of censure. What was more, the prince had no ego: he was quite happy to change his view if, in the opinion of his advisers, that view was wrong. The implication, to the listening Henry IV, was obvious: praise for the prince's willingness to take counsel was a way of criticizing his father for failing to do so. The Commons, it was clear, were already looking forward to the day he might be king.

The prince himself faced a dilemma. While the Commons were adamant that he should return to Wales 'with all possible haste', from his perspective it was preferable to stay in London in case his father died.[26] Even though the dynastic threats had subsided, it was wise to be close at hand to prevent any disruption to his possible accession. Perhaps, too, he was concerned about an act, passed by Parliament that June, which stipulated that, on Henry IV's death, the crown should pass to Henry and then to his male heirs – but if he had no male heirs, then the successor should be his brother Thomas. This may have made him less keen to expose himself to danger in Wales, especially when his father was ill. There are signs already that Thomas was his father's favourite and that relations between Henry and his eldest younger brother were lukewarm.

Whether or not Prince Henry ended up going to Wales is unclear – his movements at this time, and over the following years, remain difficult to trace. But in October 1406, perhaps at his instigation, the laws of succession were changed: now, the crown would pass to Henry and then any heirs of Henry's body, not simply males. The odds of his brother Thomas succeeding to the throne had – in theory – substantially lengthened, which was presumably exactly what Henry had in mind. And he was definitely present at a contentious royal council meeting of 8 December that year, in which a wide-ranging discussion both of the king's itinerary – which the council took the liberty of dictating, at least in part – and of royal government was held.[27] The meeting resulted in thirty-one articles being put forward in Parliament that month for governmental reform, which included a request that 'all items and matters passed by the council should be passed by all those of the council in person'.[28] The emphasis was clearly on consultation and collective responsibility.

Prince Henry's regular inclusion in the royal council for the first time was a sign not only of his growing political importance, especially in the context of his father's deteriorating health, but also of efforts to bring men of higher status into government. The Commons in 1406 had shown disquiet at Henry IV's tendency to use more lowly knights and esquires and at his spending so much on patronage of those within his circle. By involvement in the council and in the response to the Commons' requests for reform, the prince was also indicating his support for efforts to cut costs and end corruption and favouritism. Thereafter, as Henry IV's reign progressed, the prince became increasingly critical in public of his father's rule, and increasingly impatient to assume the throne himself.

The following year, however, the prince was briefly in Wales for the siege of Aberystwyth, which he intended to conduct in such a way that it would be seen as a major symbol of English recovery, but his handling of it proved a disaster. While Henry IV had been harsh in his treatment of the Welsh, his son wanted to be seen to be merciful. Therefore he offered a treaty of composition. If Glyndŵr did not come to rescue the town and give battle, then the defenders would surrender without the need to give hostages. The prince had relics brought to the siege by his friend, the cleric Richard Courtenay, for the mutual oath taking. Henry's clemency turned out to be completely misguided. With no royal army encamped around Aberystwyth, Glyndŵr entered the town and expelled those who had made the agreement. Aberystwyth was not taken by the English until September 1408 and by others, not the prince. Although the prince continued to hold the royal lieutenancy in Wales into 1410, he chose not to play a direct role, basing himself in Worcester and Hereford when not in London. Anticipating that he might become king any day, he therefore needed to be close to the centre of government.

Other matters were occupying him now. At the end of 1407, the French, beset by deepening internal divisions following the assassination of Louis, Duke of Orléans at the behest of John the Fearless, Duke of Burgundy, were keen to reopen negotiations with the English, including the prospect of marriage for the prince. Although nothing came of this, it was increasingly apparent that, with the French king suffering from mental illness, factional infighting in France would continue. The assassination of Duke Louis, the king's brother, had given the Burgundians the upper hand at this stage. The English, including the prince, watched the situation with interest.

Prince Henry attended the royal council often in 1408 and carried considerable influence within it. His lack of affection for his brother Thomas is surely reflected in the council's decision in August that the latter should no longer be a charge on the king's household, while a year later,

Thomas was replaced as lieutenant in Ireland by the steward of the prince's household, Sir John Stanley. The growing influence of Prince Henry on royal policy and his interest in military provision are also revealed by his appointment as Constable of Dover and Warden of the Cinque Ports on 28 February 1409. Around the same time, he was given custody of Edmund Mortimer, Earl of March, and his brother, as well as the keeping of their estates since they were both minors. With Henry IV increasingly concerned that he might not have much longer to live – he drew up his will on 21 January 1409 – it was sensible for his heir to have control of a possible rival claimant to the throne.

That autumn, Prince Henry spent much time with the king at his manor of Berkhamstead, expecting his father's end to be imminent. The prince was increasingly frustrated: his father's ill-health had left the crown at an impasse – he had appeared to be on the verge of death for a number of years – and things came to a head in December, when the prince took matters into his own hands and began to chair the council in his father's absence. There were major disputes between the prince and the old guard over what should be given priority. He forced his father's councillors to resign – the treasurer, Sir John Tiptoft, and the chancellor, Archbishop Arundel, the latter being a particularly close associate of the king and opposed to the reforms and changes which the prince supported – and introduced his own nominees to office, Henry, Lord Scrope as treasurer and Sir Thomas Beaufort as chancellor. He had the parliament intended to meet in Bristol switched to Westminster. In this parliament, which began on 27 January 1410, fully one-sixth of its members were connected to the prince; it was opened by his half-uncle and ally Henry Beaufort, Bishop of Winchester, brother of the chancellor.

Throughout this parliament, the prince's reformist agenda shines through. The articles presented by the Commons on 23 April 1410 included matters close to his heart, such as the costs of the household, enforcement of legislation, and law and order. During this parliament, a restriction was also placed on the king's authority. Although its precise nature is uncertain, it hardly endeared young Henry's take-over to the sick king, and nor, we can imagine, did the prince's cutting of expenses of the household and suspension of some annuities.

In this reformist atmosphere, it cannot be a coincidence that a bill for disendowment of the Church was put forward at the parliament by Lollard sympathizers – knights and esquires who followed the teachings of John Wycliffe. With an emphasis on Bible-centred fundamentalism, they challenged the Church's teaching on the sacraments as well as the special authority of the clergy and papacy. They believed that the Church had been corrupted by its involvement in secular affairs and by its extensive landholdings: hence they sought in the petition of 1410 to redistribute its possessions in order to fund more worthy causes such as almshouses, the defence of the realm and even an expansion in the number of lords, knights and esquires. Henry had friends who were sympathetic to new ideas in religion and they were emboldened by his dominance of the government and by a belief that he was open-minded enough to allow at least debate. Nothing came of the petition, but Henry had not shown himself as hostile to its sympathizers. When John Badby was condemned as a heretic by the Bishop of Worcester for denying transubstantiation (that the bread and wine actually did become the body and blood of Christ in the sacrament of communion) and was handed over for burning in March 1410, the prince had attended in person and made every effort to persuade Badby to repent, even halting the burning briefly when he believed he heard Badby wishing to do so.

Throughout 1410 and for most of the following year, the prince's dominance continued unchallenged. He brought into the council more of his own associates, including the Earls of Arundel and Warwick, and Henry Chichele, Bishop of St David's, while council meetings were held in unorthodox venues, such as friends' houses and the prince's own dwelling at Coldharbour. Dispensing with the usual protocols, Prince Henry was visibly distancing himself from his father. An expectation that it would not be too long before he became king is reflected in the presentation to the prince by the English chancery clerk and poet Thomas Hoccleve, some time between November 1410 and November 1411, of *The Regiment of Princes*, a work in the tradition of 'mirrors for princes' which suggested ways of good rule.[29] Henry had a similar but shorter work in Latin, *De Officio Militari* ('On the Military Office'), written for him by Richard Ullerstone of Queen's College, Oxford, at the behest of Richard Courtenay during the latter's tenure of the chancellorship of Oxford between June 1406 and September 1411.[30]

The prince's ascendancy is evidenced in foreign policy,

too. In July 1410, the council agreed that financial priority should be given to the prince for the defence of Calais, then under threat of French attack. Having already argued for the importance of this isolated English outpost in France at the council in December 1409, the prince had made himself Captain of Calais on 18 March 1410 and had ensured that 75 per cent of the wool subsidy granted at the parliament should be earmarked to the wages of the garrison. In France, however, divisions were worsening between John the Fearless, Duke of Burgundy, then in control of the royal government in the light of the French king's incapacity, and his Orléanist enemies. Charles, Duke of Orléans – son of Louis, whose assassination John the Fearless had orchestrated in 1407 – had built up a group of supporters. These became known as the Armagnacs through Duke Charles's marriage to the daughter of the Count of Armagnac, and included several leading peers. By 1410, the situation was sliding into civil war. In August 1411, Duke John approached the English for an alliance 'by way of marriage between my lord the prince and the eldest daughter of the duke', a reiteration of the proposal of 1407 but this time in return for military support against his enemies.[31]

Prince Henry was not slow to spot an opportunity: specifically, gaining Burgundian support for the recovery of English lands in France. The central tenet of English policy towards France remained an insistence on the terms which Edward III had negotiated in 1360 in the Treaty of Brétigny, often known to the English as 'the Great Peace' – with good reason. This treaty had given English kings a substantial swathe of sovereign territory in south-west France, but from the end of the 1360s onwards, with Edward III no longer the force he had been and then under the boy-king Richard II, most of these territorial gains had been lost. Now, in 1411, the deal which Prince Henry struck with Duke John reflected his lack of experience in foreign affairs: it was vague and open-ended, requiring no firm guarantee of Burgundian help for the recovery of the lands of the Treaty of Brétigny. Yet Henry was committed to the treaty, presumably because he saw it as a way of dissuading Duke John from attacking Calais. That October, the prince sent English troops under the prince's close friend Thomas Fitzalan, Earl of Arundel, to help the Burgundians recover Saint-Cloud, near Paris, which they did on 9 November. Tellingly, these troops were not funded from the royal Exchequer but from the prince's own revenues in his earldom of Chester, an indication that the ailing king had not been in agreement with his son's plans.[32]

Increasing concerns about young Henry's actions as well as an apparent improvement in his health led to the king planning to take back control of government. But tensions escalated. The prince tried and failed in September 1411 to protect Richard Courtenay, in his role as Chancellor of Oxford, against the visitation rights of Archbishop Arundel, which threatened the independence of the university as well as the authority of its chancellor. In the following month, six of the prince's household knights, including his steward, Sir Roger Leche, were arrested. Around the opening of Parliament on 3 November 1411, the prince appears to have confronted his father, saying that he should abdicate, as he 'could no longer work for the honour and utility of the kingdom'.[33] A proposal seems to have been put to the Lords by the prince and Henry Beaufort 'as to which of them would ask the king if he was prepared to resign the crown of England and allow his first-born son to be crowned'.[34]

Rejecting these approaches, the king took swift action. On 30 November, the prince and the royal council he had assembled were publicly sacked in Parliament. The speech the prince gave in response reminded the king waspishly 'that they would have been able to do their duty better' had they been given more funds and support: the prince was openly criticizing the king and the old guard for their opposition to his reforms and his foreign policy.[35] On 19 December, the last day of the parliament, the king quashed the restriction which had been placed on his royal prerogative in the previous parliament. The prince's associates Henry, Lord Scrope and Thomas Beaufort were dismissed from their posts as treasurer and chancellor respectively on the following day. Sir John Pelham, a long-standing member of the king's duchy of Lancaster staff and Treasurer of War in 1404–6, was appointed treasurer, and on 5 January 1412 Archbishop Arundel was reappointed as chancellor. The new council contained none of the prince's associates.

The prince was cast into the political wilderness. Relations with his father worsened in the spring of 1412 when the king responded positively to an approach by the Armagnac faction in France for military support against the Burgundians. In the subsequent treaty, signed at Bourges on 18 May, the Armagnacs acknowledged all English rights of the Great Peace and, furthermore, offered to assist Henry IV in his 'just quarrels' with the King of France in return for military support – an army of 4,000 men – and a promise not to enter into any alliance with the Duke of Burgundy. Yet in practice the king showed himself as naïve as the prince had been in 1411: the Armagnacs were not in control of Charles VI and could not turn their promises into reality. Furthermore, by the time the English troops arrived in France on 10 August, the Armagnacs and Burgundians were already negotiating a peace with each other, which was finally sealed at Auxerre on 22 August 1412.

Henry IV had hoped to lead the army to France himself, but by 8 June illness forced his delegating of command to his second son, Thomas, whom he created Duke of Clarence on 9 July. Prince Henry's relations with his brother had now reached a very low ebb. While in control of the council in June 1410, he had already refused to pay Thomas the arrears due him as Lieutenant of Ireland until he demonstrated that he had fulfilled the terms of his contract – the implication being that his brother's word could not be trusted. Now he was completely outraged by the preference being shown by his father to Thomas, whose position had also been strengthened by his marriage in November 1411 to Margaret Holland, widow of the king's half-brother John Beaufort, Earl of Somerset, and niece of Archbishop Arundel. In addition, Prince Henry was embarrassed by having to write to the Duke of Burgundy in late May to explain that he had had no choice but to accept his father's decision to support the Armagnacs.

On 17 June, a week or so after Henry IV had publicly

delegated command of the army to his second son, the prince issued a public letter from his manor of Cheylesmore in Coventry. He had been willing to go on the campaign, he claimed, but his father had suggested that he go with such a small force 'that the king had made it impossible for us to serve him with honour or to make effective provision for the proper safety of our person'. The king, Prince Henry insinuated, had deliberately engineered Thomas's command of the army. Moreover, he added, 'certain sons of iniquity' had sown rumours that he was trying to disrupt the expedition. These people, he claimed, were desiring 'to attack the proper order of succession', the implication being that they were planning to set him aside in preference of his brother Thomas.[36] Prince Henry took care to name no names, but, reading between the lines, it is clear that rumours were rife that he was planning a coup against his father.

Around the end of June, the prince came to London 'with a considerable company of friends and a large retinue of men in his service such as had not been seen before in those days', a reminder – if indeed anybody now needed reminding – of the fact that he had a large affinity of armed men at his disposal. The king delayed admitting him to his presence but finally did so, according to Thomas Walsingham, 'welcoming him with open arms'.[37] *The First English Life of King Henry V* gives a colourful account of this meeting: although written in 1513, a century after the event, it may have some basis in reality since the anonymous author had at his disposal reminiscences of the 4th Earl of Ormond, who had known Henry V. Here the prince comes to the king wearing a blue robe full of eyelet holes, each with a needle hanging from it. (The meaning of such a garment is unknown: perhaps the holes and needles were intended to symbolize that the prince was not a 'finished product'.) The prince fell to his knees and offered a dagger with which the king might kill him: 'my life is not so desirous to me that I would live one day that I should be to your displeasure'.[38]

Even so, the king gave an obtuse answer to the prince's request that 'those who had denounced him should be punished if they could be found guilty', saying that such a procedure should await the next meeting of Parliament 'so that men such as these might be punished after judgement by their peers'.[39] The king, clearly, did not see the need for action as urgently as Prince Henry did: it took him the best part of six months to issue summons for a parliament to meet on 3 February 1413.

Meanwhile, the council had taken the opportunity to investigate other charges against the prince that he had been involved in peculation, embezzling the wages of the Calais garrison. This inquiry took three months, from July to September, and the prince was not fully exonerated until 21 October. He tried to put pressure on the king again in September by coming to London with a large retinue. There may even have been an assassination attempt against the prince at this point (or so it was claimed in 1426). But amid the rumours of plot and counter-plot, the king's state of health continued to decline. The opening of Parliament planned for 3 February was postponed. On 20 March, Henry IV finally passed away, dying in the Jerusalem Chamber in the abbot's lodging at Westminster Abbey.

To what extent father and son were ever fully reconciled

during Henry IV's lifetime is difficult to assess: a deathbed scene is found in so many narratives that it cannot be dismissed as simply invention, although it was coloured by how Henry V chose to transform himself after his accession. Both of the Latin lives of Henry V describe the dying king giving his blessing to his son before telling us of acts of contrition by the prince, lamenting his past bad behaviour. *The First English Life* also gives an extended scene around Henry IV's deathbed in which the king expresses his concern that, after his passing, discord would arise between the prince and his brother Thomas. The prince reassures him otherwise, and in a long oration his father gives him his blessing.[40] Stories of a deathbed reunion also spread abroad. Burgundian chronicles written in the mid fifteenth century claimed that Henry had been seen by his dying father trying on the crown but that this led to an act of contrition by the prince and the forgiveness of his father.[41] Closer to the event, we have a letter to his son supposedly written by Henry IV on his deathbed, and recited in a work attributed to Thomas Elmham.[42] This was very much in the mode of a model for princes, urging the prince to honour God and protect his people.

By the early sixteenth century, stories of the prince's ill-spent youth were popular and were subsequently taken up by Shakespeare. In reality there is no evidence from the period itself of the prince behaving as Hal did. Stories of his criminal tendencies and his arrest by Chief Justice Gascoigne were sixteenth-century inventions (although he did indeed remove Gascoigne from office on his accession). But the two Latin lives say intriguing things about Prince Henry.

The Pseudo-Elmham, for instance, speaks of the prince as 'an assiduous pursuer of fun, devoted to organ instruments [an intentional double entendre] which relaxed the rein on his modesty; although under the military service of Mars, he seethed youthfully with the flames of Venus too, and tended to be open to other novelties as befitted the age of his untamed youth'.[43] Since these sit awkwardly in what are otherwise adulatory texts, and both works have links with men who knew Henry well, we should give them some credence.

There are other signs of the prince's enthusiasm for novelty. He owned the earliest-known manuscript of Chaucer's racy *Troilus and Criseyde*, acquired some time between 1406 and 1413.[44] His keenness for works in English is also seen in his commissioning of John Lydgate in October 1412 to write the *Troy Book*, although the poem was not completed until 1420, and of the dedication to him, when prince, of a translation into English of Gaston Fébus's *Livre de chasse* by his cousin Edward, Duke of York. The latter work remained important to him, since he commissioned twelve copies of it as gifts in November 1421.[45] His youthful energy, which no doubt contributed to his sense of frustration in waiting for his sickly father to die, is also suggested in the Latin lives, which speak of him as having a long neck and a graceful and strong but not muscular body, with an excellent turn of speed when running to catch deer.[46] Although we have evidence of expenditure on a 'hastilude of peace' (a form of tournament) at his manor of Kennington at Christmas 1409,[47] there is no evidence of his ever participating in person in a joust. As king, his associates seem to have been keen to send wrestlers to entertain him, perhaps reflecting his enthusiasm for the sport.[48]

What cannot be doubted is that Prince Henry was impatient to become king. The way he conducted affairs when in control of the government in 1410–11 suggests that he did not always conform to expected patterns of political behaviour – witness his convening of the royal council in private houses and the suspicion that he had misused funds for the Calais garrison. Relations with his father reached crisis point at the end of 1411, when he tried to force an abdication, and again in the summer of 1412, when he was believed to be attempting a coup and when his father may have considered excluding him from the succession, and may never have been fully resolved in Henry IV's lifetime. This situation led to the prince's disengagement with government in the last year or so of the reign. Such 'knowns' can be taken to suggest that the 'unknowns' of riotous behaviour and unsuitable associates are true.

2

New King, New Man

On 9 April 1413, with a snowstorm raging outside, Henry V, now aged twenty-six, was crowned King of England in Westminster Abbey. According to Thomas Walsingham, people pondered what this unseasonal 'turbulence of the elements' might indicate about the new king's reign. Some, reported Walsingham, took it to mean that he would be 'cold in his deeds and harsh in his rule'; others – 'more wisely', Walsingham qualified – 'interpreted the intemperance in the weather as an excellent omen, saying that the king would make the snows and frosts of vices in the kingdom disappear and the austere fruits of virtue appear so that it could truly be said by his subjects, "Now the winter has passed, the rain is over and gone"'. Walsingham went on to clarify his reasoning: as soon as Henry took on the mantle of kingship, he immediately changed into a different person, 'dedicated to honour, propriety and dignity of demeanour ... his behaviour and bearing seemed to be appropriate to every situation that would foster acts of virtue, and men considered themselves fortunate to be able to follow his example'.[1]

That Henry consciously transformed himself on his accession is found in other texts, although none composed so early in the reign as Walsingham's account, which was written roughly contemporaneously with events. Both of the Latin lives of the king emphasize the change. For Tito Livio, Henry 'profoundly corrected his life and habits so that after his father's death no element of lasciviousness was ever found in him'. For the Pseudo-Elmham, the change was so complete that 'left was changed into right'.[2] From what we know of Henry's behaviour in the last years of his father's reign, and his actions and demeanour in the early phases of his own, he does indeed appear to have consciously made himself a changed man at his accession, conducting himself with a gravitas that reflected his commitment to his new role as king. Such a deliberate step on becoming king would seem to confirm his previous unruly behaviour: what he could permit in himself as prince he could not allow himself as king. Henry V, in other words, had a strong personal concept of kingship.

Throughout his reign, he took the responsibilities of kingship seriously, even obsessively, an approach perhaps to be expected of someone who had waited for several frustrating years to become king and who had become increasingly critical of his predecessor. And given what had happened in recent years, Henry had a lot to prove. His reform was inextricably bound up with his desire to establish his position as king. Henry needed to boost his own reputation both internally and externally. A change of ruler was always an uncertain time and in this case the dynasty itself was still young. His own princely record in war and politics was less than impressive. His conscious transformation of himself was also shaped by guilt and remorse about his relationship with his father.

Religion played a strong part here. In brief, Henry turned to God and the Church at this key moment of his life. As an anointed king, chosen and blessed by God, Henry believed that his actions were inspired and guided by divine will. Any successes were not his but God's. As God's servant, he had a strong sense of his duty to protect and promote the Catholic faith in his kingdom. Both the Latin lives have him rushing from his father's deathbed to a monk to confess his sins and to pledge that he would reform his ways, while his choice of Carmelite friars as confessors showed his commitment to strict and theologically sophisticated guidance. Such confessors were kept constantly at hand 'en nostre houstell' ('in our household').[3] Henry V's first household account shows a formidable array of preachers brought in for the king's daily Mass, as well as 2d per day for the 'oratores regis', men who prayed on behalf of the king, in order to boost his own approaches to the Almighty.[4]

Westminster Abbey was a special place for him. He visited, and made confession to, the recluse of Westminster, William Alnwick,[5] as part of his transformative devotions on becoming king, attended several services and sermons there in the first months of his reign, and had probably already chosen the place for his burial. By the time he had made his first will, on 24 July 1415, shortly before setting out on campaign, he had devised a fully worked-out scheme. His body was to be buried among the tombs of his predecessors, with a chapel built above it into which all of the abbey's main relics were to be gathered. In order to encourage increased devotion in others, the altar of this chapel was to be positioned so that the people could see the priests celebrating Mass.[6]

Henry's religious transformation inevitably involved a moral conversion. The Latin lives tell us that he abandoned the pleasures of the flesh on becoming king. As the Pseudo-Elmham puts it: 'by a fortunate miracle ... Paris [whose desire caused the Trojan war] is converted into Hippolytus [who was killed for rejecting Phaedra's advance], sensuality into sense'.[7] The prologue to *The First English Life* further claims that from the time of his father's death to his own marriage in 1420, he practised the strictest continence, something we might dismiss as legend but for its confirmation by an independent and contemporary source. When Jean Fusoris, a canon of Notre-Dame in Paris and – as it transpired – a spy working for the English in the lead-up to the invasion of France, was later tried by the French, he told the court that he had heard from Richard Courtenay, one of Henry's closest and longest-standing friends, that since his accession the king had not had carnal relations with a woman.[8]

Fusoris also described Henry as better disposed to being a man of the Church than a soldier.[9] Throughout his reign Henry displayed a strong interest in theological works. At the death of Archbishop Arundel in 1414, for instance, the king requested sight of a volume of the works of Gregory the Great which the archbishop had bequeathed to Christ Church Priory, Canterbury, and held on to it for several years.[10] Later in the reign, he commissioned a translation from Latin into French of the Pseudo-Bonaventure *Meditationes Vitae Christi* ('Meditations on the Life of Christ'), a devotional work of Franciscan origin which clearly appealed to the king's religious taste.[11] The careful distribution of Henry's books in his wills and codicil to his monastic foundations and the University of Oxford reflect his personal knowledge of their contents and their appropriateness for each institution.[12] Furthermore, his religious devotion may even have extended to composing a Gloria and a Sanctus, both for three voices.[13] This is unlikely to have been the kind of music which the Latin lives saw as 'relaxing the rein on his modesty' as prince, and therefore constituted a further example of the marked change in him on his accession.

Later, and memorably, Henry's personal transformation on becoming king was portrayed by his rejection of the unsuitable friends of his youth. A 1479 version of the *Brut Chronicle*, printed in English by William Caxton, tells the story of Henry summoning his household immediately after his accession. They came 'winking and smiling ... thinking they would get great offices'.[14] Some he paid off and ordered not to come into his presence again, and at least fourteen of his former retainers are not found in his service as king. By contrast, those of his entourage considered suitable were appointed to high positions. One of Henry's military associates as prince, Thomas Fitzalan, Earl of Arundel, was appointed treasurer, replacing Sir John Pelham, while he made Henry Beaufort his chancellor, replacing Archbishop Arundel, one of the principal critics of his behaviour as prince. Other regular members of his royal council, such as Thomas Langley, Bishop of Durham, had, like Beaufort, also worked with Henry during his period in control of the council in 1410–11. These included two men he now promoted as soon as possible to bishoprics: his friend Richard

Courtenay, who became Bishop of Norwich in June 1413, and Henry Chichele, made Archbishop of Canterbury at the death of Arundel in February 1414.

As prince, Henry's relations with his brother Thomas, Duke of Clarence had not been good. As king, Henry treated his brother with honour, but removing him from the key role of Captain of Calais in February 1414, in favour of the Earl of Warwick, suggests that he preferred to put his trust in others.[15] Like the Earl of Arundel, Warwick was highly trusted by Henry, who gave him an important diplomatic role in negotiations with France and at the Council of Constance, a highly significant international summit that opened in November 1414 in an attempt to resolve the schism between rival popes which had divided Europe since 1378. Henry was keen to have an independent English presence recognized at this Church council, rather than being subsumed within the broader 'German' nation which supported the Roman pope, thereby strengthening his own hand against the French who supported the Avignon claimant.

Despite bringing in his own allies, Henry did not conduct a purge of his father's men but chose to retain those he knew he could trust. Sir Thomas Erpingham, appointed steward of the household on 23 March 1413, was a long associate of the Lancastrian regime, serving both John of Gaunt and Henry IV, whom he had also served as steward. Henry's choice for the equally important office of chamberlain of the household was Henry, Lord Fitzhugh, who had been one of Henry IV's king's knights, a special honour accorded to those close to the sovereign. Fitzhugh was at least fifty years of age in 1413, Erpingham several years older, and both were Knights of the Garter, a clear indication of their military standing. Henry V's choice of two 'father figures' to supervise the royal household is again suggestive of his desire to project an image of good conduct, contrasting with his image as prince.

Henry was determined to be guided and supported by serious-minded and incorruptible advisers, men who reflected the style of kingship to which he had committed himself. Neither at this point nor later did he have favourites or advance anyone who did not demonstrate the high standards of probity and loyalty he expected. He was conservative in his use of patronage, expecting reward to be earned, and parsimonious in his creation of peerages. Although, at the parliament of May 1414, he elevated his brothers John and Humphrey to ducal status (Bedford and Gloucester) and his cousin Richard to Earl of Cambridge, these were not well supported with lands and revenues and were granted for life only, again an expression of the need even for members of his family to show their worth. But where loyalty was proven, he rewarded it. As prince, Henry had supported his cousin Edward, Duke of York when doubts had been cast on the latter's loyalty by Henry IV. As king, he took pains to have the parliament of May 1414 declare the duke to be free of suspicion, acknowledging him as 'a good liege to his father and to himself, and wishing him to be regarded as such'.[16]

Mindful of the financial problems that dogged his father's reign, Henry kept the size and costs of his household low. Nor did his reign see the frequent chopping and changing in office-holding which his father's had witnessed: a lower turnover indicated a king who was sure of his judgement and clear in his intentions. Conscious of the criticism his father had attracted for promoting men of low rank, Henry was keen to have leading nobles and clergy as the core of his council. The militarism of his reign generated by the wars with France assisted in bringing peers and leading knights into the king's inner circle.

Henry was a 'hands-on' monarch, anxious to make his mark in all areas of business, especially in ensuring good justice, public order and financial probity and in promoting England's standing in Europe, but it was a mark of a good king to take counsel, both from the regular royal council as well as from great councils and Parliament. Three days after he was crowned, in a sign of his return from the political wilderness to which he had been relegated before his accession, he arranged an unprecedented personal meeting with the nobles and knights at which he promised to rule for the honour of God and the prosperity of the realm. Those present in turn swore oaths of allegiance to him as king.[17] By this ceremony he sought to expunge any lingering doubts on his inheritance in the light of his alleged attempted coup and his father's apparent preference for his brother Thomas. As a public gesture, and demonstrating his adherence to expected royal practice at a new accession, the king indicated his intention to issue a general pardon, having messengers sent out on the day of his coronation to proclaim it.[18] These actions publicized his good intentions, but the political nation still needed time to discover what kind of a king he would be.

A few weeks after his accession, he had publicly announced that Richard II would receive a royal reburial in Westminster Abbey, and in early December he fulfilled the promise. It was an astute move. In bringing Richard to Westminster from his initial burial place at the Dominican Friary at King's Langley – and, what was more, reburying him in the tomb that Richard had previously reserved for himself – the king aimed (unsuccessfully, as it turned out) both to quash rumours, circulating for over a decade, that Richard was still alive and living in Scotland; it also gave Henry the chance to pay his respects publicly to a king who had behaved honourably towards him in Ireland until his father's invasion. Henry V even borrowed the banners used for his own father's burial in June at Canterbury Cathedral – underscoring the new king's keenness to draw the line under past conflicts while at the same time emphasizing the legitimacy and magnificence of his dynastic forbears and thereby himself.[19]

His father's funeral was itself a spectacular event, the king ordering ninety flags bearing the arms of all Christian kings and other leading men and fifty with the images of heroes as a sign of Henry IV's place in the panoply of famous men. The candles at the vigil and ceremony cost the king £100, with a further £160 being expended on a single item – a golden bejewelled head to be given as an offering to the shrine of Thomas Becket.[20] Henry's reverence for his dead father is also witnessed in his cherishing of the latter's breviary and Great Bible. Although he subsequently lent the latter to his Bridgettine foundation at Sheen, he made clear in his last will that it should be returned at his death to his royal successor.[21]

In May 1413, with the same mixture of personal devotion and dynastic publicity, he had commissioned a new effigy for his mother's tomb in Leicester, with 'divers arms of the king of England', even though she had died five years before her husband seized the throne.[22] He also made other gestures of reconciliation early in his reign, releasing from house arrest Edmund, Earl of March, a possible rival claimant to the throne given his descent from the second son of Edward III. By the authority of Parliament, the earl was given full control of his estates on 9 June 1413.[23]

On the day of his accession, Henry issued writs for a parliament to meet on 15 May. The new king had to live up to the commitment to sound financial management he had shown when in control of government in 1410–11. Fully aware of the financial difficulties that had plagued his father's reign, Henry V was wise at his first parliament to promise that the funding of the royal household would take priority over the payment of other external costs, including annuities distributed as royal patronage. This linked back to one of the articles put forward by the Commons in April 1410, thereby showing a deliberate continuity in his policies between his period in government as prince and his early actions as king.[24] By showing he was 'willing to accommodate the wishes of the Commons and giving an indication of serious intent to rein in royal extravagance', he reaped the reward: the Commons granted him taxes on wool exports for four years as well as a lay subsidy, the standard form of direct taxation in late medieval England.[25]

That the Commons were aware of unfulfilled past royal

promises is shown in the petition they made to the king and Lords on 22 May 1413. The Speaker recalled that, in the time of Henry IV, 'the Commons had requested good governance on many occasions and their requests had been granted but our lord the king was well aware of how this had been subsequently fulfilled and carried out'. This was a euphemistic way of saying that Henry IV had promised much but delivered little. The Speaker went on to hope that 'since God had endowed the new king with good sense and many other bounties and virtues', he would practise and maintain good governance.[26]

Henry V had been critical of his father in 1410–11 and those present would have known that. But now he was king, he could not be seen as simply responding to the Commons' criticisms: he had to take charge while at the same time indicating that he was willing to listen. Therefore he told the Commons to put their concerns in writing rather than immediately agreeing to their demands at the parliament. The list of issues presented covered almost everything: from Ireland, Wales, the Scottish marches, Calais, Gascony, and the keeping of the sea and lack of a navy, to provision for the resistance of enemies, good governance and obedience to the law.[27]

That he took lawlessness as a particularly urgent matter – hardly surprising for a new and energetic king committed to establishing God's kingdom on earth – is seen in the second parliament of his reign, held at Leicester in April and May 1414. The tone was set by the opening speech of Henry Beaufort in which he explained how the king had 'always fully committed himself to living and existing under the most commendable precepts and governance of the most holy law of God ... considering that a kingdom cannot be in a state of well-being without omnipotent God being praised and honoured first and foremost and above all things'. We see clearly the image which Henry aimed to project as a model king, directed by God. The chancellor added that the king was keen to 'make new laws for the ease and benefit of his lieges ... particularly for the chastisement and punishment of rioters, murderers and other malefactors who now abound in various parts of the kingdom'.[28] A crackdown on such behaviour would demonstrate the new king's authority.

In the Statute of Riots which came out of the April 1414 parliament, drafted under the guidance of the king and his advisers, although technically at the request of the Commons, the king referred back to a statute of 1411, as a reminder that he had always been tough on law and order (implicitly, in contrast with his father). Furthermore, he showed he was a man of action as well as words by sending out the King's Bench for special sessions in the counties bordering Wales where the worst lawlessness had been occurring. He was astute in not asking the Commons for direct taxation at this second parliament: as the opening speech explained, the removal of this burden was 'in the hope that he will find them more willing and amenable to him and his needs in time to come'.[29] His mind was already turning to a possible reopening of war with France.

By the time of the Leicester parliament in April 1414, there had emerged another problem linked to law and order, the revolt of the condemned heretic Sir John Oldcastle in

January 1414. Sir John had served in the Welsh wars and on the expedition which Prince Henry had sent to France in 1411 under the Earl of Arundel. Oldcastle remained firmly in the royal circle after the accession, providing a group of wrestlers for the king's entertainment at Windsor on 1 August 1413 even when he was already under scrutiny by the Church for his Lollard views.[30] Two months earlier, in June, churchmen had visited Henry at Kennington (he used this princely palace on several occasions, even after his accession) and read out charges against Oldcastle. Initially Henry was reluctant to take action against his associate but, mindful of his religious duty as king, he agreed to proceedings.[31] Tried for heresy that October, Oldcastle was found guilty and handed over to the royal authorities. Even then the king hesitated and gave him forty days to reconsider – at which point Oldcastle promptly escaped from the Tower and planned an uprising.

The rebels devised an elaborate plan, proposing to disguise themselves as players and to infiltrate the royal court, then at Eltham Manor, during the Twelfth Night celebrations, and to capture Henry and his brothers. This plot, as well as plans for a larger-scale muster of Lollard sympathizers at St Giles Fields on 9 January 1414, was betrayed by two would-be conspirators, enabling the king to intercept the rebel contingents as they made for the muster point, although Oldcastle was not himself apprehended. This was a small-scale rising, with no more than 300 involved and only 69 condemned of whom 38 were put to death.[32] The king showed his keenness to conciliate: on 28 March, he offered a general pardon. With hindsight, the Lollard rebellion had not posed a major threat to the king, but it is interesting to note that one of the men involved, Sir Thomas Chaworth, had been among those whose arrest in the autumn of 1411 was probably linked to the prince's plan to force his father to abdicate.[33] In other words, Oldcastle was not the only friend of Henry who had Lollard sympathies. Chaworth was pardoned by the king and served on the 1415 campaign to France.

In the wake of the rebellion, and despite his relative leniency towards its perpetrators, Henry went out of his way to stress his religious orthodoxy all the more and to prove himself a firm supporter of the Church. As part of his law-and-order reforms at the Leicester parliament that spring, the Statute of Lollards was passed, giving justices of the peace more responsibility in supporting the Church in the detection of heresy. For the Lollards, however, Henry had clearly gone over to the dark side. A sense that they considered him hypocritical is found in the nickname they devised for him: 'the prince of priests' ('princeps presbiterorum').[34] Oldcastle's dim view of Henry is revealed in the statement he made at his trial, after his final capture in November 1417, that 'he had no judge amongst them while his liege lord Richard was still living in Scotland'.[35] His exploitation of the notion that Richard had survived indicates that Henry's reinterment of the king's body had not convinced everyone that the dynastic question was closed.

Henry's foundation of new monastic houses might very probably have been another way of removing any notion that he was sympathetic to opponents of the established Church. The chronicler Thomas Walsingham suggests as much, placing his account of Henry's monastic foundations immediately after his report on the Leicester parliament. (In this context, it is also worth remembering that the Lollards had been particularly critical of monasticism.) One foundation, a Carthusian house founded on 1 April 1415, was placed close to the royal manor of Sheen, the site of the palace which Richard II had demolished in grief following the death of his first wife. Intended as a house of prayer for the Lancastrian dynasty, it was thereby an element in his posthumous reconciliation with his father. Henry may also have seen the foundation as fulfilling the penance imposed on Henry IV in 1408 by the pope for the execution of Archbishop Scrope after his rebellion against the king in 1405.[36] Another house, this time accommodating nuns of the Bridgettine Order, was originally founded at Isleworth on 22 February 1415, later moving to a site directly across the Thames from Henry's Carthusian monastery at Sheen, and named Syon.

In favouring the Bridgettines – founded in Sweden – Henry showed himself to be fully up to date in his religiosity: the house was for both men and women, the latter to devote themselves to study, the former to preaching. The influence of Henry's chamberlain, Henry, Lord Fitzhugh, is apparent. Having visited Sweden in the train of Henry's sister Philippa, when she crossed the North Sea to marry the King of Denmark in 1406, Fitzhugh had been impressed enough to offer his own lands in Cambridgeshire for a Bridgettine house, with Henry IV also showing interest in the order. The name Syon, from the biblical Mount Zion, the holy site in Jerusalem, reflected Henry V's religious aspirations: as the house's

foundation charter emphasized, it had been chosen by
Henry, 'true son of the God of peace, who gave peace and
taught peace and chose St Bridget as a lover of peace and
tranquillity'.[37] Indeed, so committed to peace was Henry
that, at this time, he was planning a war with France for the
sake of achieving it.

At the moment of Henry's accession, the English exped-
itionary army sent to France by Henry IV in the summer of
1412 to assist the Armagnac faction in its struggle against
John, Duke of Burgundy, then in control of Charles VI's
government, was still in Bordeaux, the capital of English
territory in south-west France. Although the intended joint
offensive had been aborted when the two parties in the
French civil war had made their peace at Auxerre on
22 August 1412, the English still hoped to use the troops to
strengthen the frontiers of English Gascony. The principal
commander, Henry's brother Thomas, Duke of Clarence,
had returned home once he heard of his father's death, but
Henry V kept Thomas Beaufort, Earl of Dorset, in Bordeaux, ordering a campaign into Saintonge (the coastal
area north of Gascony) to follow up Thomas's earlier
actions in the Angoumois (the region around Angoulême).
Henry was fully aware of the promises made to him and his
father by both sides in the civil war in 1411–12 that in
return for English military support they would assist in the
recovery of the lands given to Edward III in the Treaty of
Brétigny of 1360, but he also knew that the Armagnacs and
Burgundians were now united. Therefore his main concern
was to renew the Anglo-French truce which had been in
place since 1396. Since treaties and truces were between

rulers in person, such a renewal was required at the accession of a new king. On 29 June 1413, Henry Chichele, Bishop of St David's, prepared a memorandum for the king about the diplomatic position: based on this advice, Henry appointed Chichele and others to negotiate the renewal of the truce.

The truce was confirmed on 23 September and again on 24 January 1414, but the French chose to keep each renewal short, initially adopting an aggressive stance towards Henry as a new, and in their opinion, inexperienced and insecure ruler. Yet divisions in France were re-emerging. The efforts of John, Duke of Burgundy to exploit popular support in Paris had misfired and he was forced to flee the capital. This left the royal government in the hands of his enemies, the Armagnac faction. By February 1414, Duke John had been declared a traitor and full civil war was reignited, with royal troops attacking his lands in Picardy, in north-eastern France.

While Henry appeared to approach the talks with an open mind, it became increasingly apparent that the divisions in France offered fresh opportunity to boost English interests. Both the Duke of Burgundy and the French king were offering Henry the prospect of marriage in exchange for an active English alliance – and Henry, a bachelor, needed to marry and to get on with the business of producing heirs. What was more, he had received promising reports from the Duke of York, in Paris in August 1413, of the 'beauty, grace and good demeanour' of Catherine, thirteen-year-old daughter of the French king, Charles VI.[38]

On 28 January 1414, Henry empowered Henry, Lord

Scrope and others to treat for a peace with France focused on a marriage to Catherine, with the promise that until 1 May he would not contract marriage with anyone else.[39] But with full-blown civil war erupting in France that summer, Henry saw a chance to press his claims further, hoping not only for a generous dowry for Catherine but also negotiated territorial gains based on the Treaty of Brétigny which would extend English lands in south-west France. In May, Burgundian envoys had arrived in England while Parliament was sitting, and had entered into talks for an Anglo-Burgundian alliance against France. As prince, Henry had been hopeful that Duke John could help English interests in France, but now the duke had lost control of the French government, the English concluded that he was 'promising more than he could deliver or . . . more than he intended'.[40]

A report drawn up by Thierry Gherbode, one of the envoys commissioned in June 1414 to negotiate a Burgundian marriage for Henry, argued forcefully against any deal with England. His argument was that Henry was not the legitimate king of England as his father had been a usurper and there was a better claimant to the throne descended from the second son of Edward III who, 'come the hour, would show himself'.[41] The envoy was certainly keen to dig up the supposed dirt on Henry, claiming even that his mother had been a professed nun whose husband had abducted her to benefit from her landed inheritance. The Chinese whispers of history are apparent: although the allegation of sexual impropriety was patently false, there was an element of truth in that Henry's mother was a co-heiress to extremely valuable landholdings with her sister, the Duchess of Gloucester (widow of Thomas of Woodstock, fifth son of Edward III).

In early autumn 1414, with his main focus still on negotiations with the French royal government, Henry sent a grand embassy to Paris to discuss two proposals for peace: 'the way of matrimony and affinity' and 'the way of the administration of justice and restoration of our rights and inheritance'.[42] Henry was willing to put aside his claim to the throne of France in return for the full implementation of the Brétigny settlement, which would have given him the whole of Aquitaine, Poitou and Ponthieu, the sums outstanding from the ransom of the French king John II, who had been captured at the Battle of Poitiers in 1356, and a dowry for marriage to Catherine of 2 million *écus* (around £330,000). He added, for good measure, the direct tenure of Normandy, Maine and Anjou and the overlordship of Brittany and Flanders, as well as even two areas (Beaufort and Nogent) claimed by virtue of his Lancastrian inheritance. Perhaps Henry was trying to exploit French fears of an Anglo-Burgundian alliance in order to extract maximum concessions. But maybe his aims were different: to make such high demands that the French would reject them, thereby justifying war. At this point he may have considered a military alliance with Burgundy a real option.

Unsurprisingly, the French rejected his proposals, although they did offer a substantial dowry of 600,000 *écus*. But with his sweeping demands, Henry had boxed himself into a corner, and risked losing face if he did not react to French rejections of his claims. At the same time, he was aware of the possible advantage of attacking while the French were divided. Therefore as soon as the failure of the great embassy was known, he summoned Parliament to meet on 19 November 1414. The opening speech of the chancellor, Henry Beaufort, announced the king's intention to make war on France, arguing that it was a 'suitable time' to do so – an allusion to internal divisions in France.[43] By the time the Commons came to discuss a tax to support Henry's projected war, enough fervour had been whipped up to persuade them to vote a double lay subsidy to be collected in February 1415 and February 1416, a generosity matched in the convocation of the clergy of the Canterbury province, which also agreed to levy a double tax on the clergy.

A council of nobles and gentry held during or shortly after the parliament expressed a willingness to give military service. But there was still some caution in their views. They urged that another embassy be sent to France, which was implemented in the New Year. The envoys were empowered to put forward substantially lower demands of the Brétigny lands only and a dowry of 1 million *écus*. But the embassy was overtaken by events in France. On 23 February 1415, the Burgundians and the Armagnac-controlled government agreed to patch up their differences. The French deliberately insulted the English envoys by having them present their demands on the very day, 13 March, that the factions made their public oaths for peace and reconciliation and Charles VI ordered taxation to be levied to protect the kingdom against invasion. With the threat of an Anglo-Burgundian military offensive having receded, the

French dismissed all the English demands, considering themselves strong enough to resist Henry both in diplomacy and in war.

An incident which has achieved legendary proportions because of its splendid portrayal in Shakespeare's *Henry V* is the dauphin's sending of a gift of tennis balls to Henry. That this happened is almost certainly true, and shows the view the French had of Henry as an unimpressive and unseasoned military leader. The problem is dating the gesture. According to Thomas Elmham, while Henry was in Kenilworth for Lent, 'the dauphin Charles [*recte*, Louis], son of the French king, wrote to him very jesting words and sent Paris balls with which he could play with his young men, as was his wont'. The king's reply was that he 'would very shortly send London balls, which would bring down their houses', promising with his own hand to win the game and put the French to flight from the kingdom.[44] Since Elmham places the account immediately after mention of the death of Archbishop Arundel (19 February 1414), the year must be 1414, where Lent began on 21 February. Government records confirm the king was at Kenilworth between late February and mid March 1414.[45]

John Strecche, a canon at Kenilworth Priory, gives a slightly different version. He has the French telling English ambassadors in Paris that they would 'send to King Henry, because he was young, little balls to play with and soft pillows to sleep on to help him grow to manly strength'. On hearing this, the king gave the same response as in Elmham, adding: 'if perchance they thought to lie abed with soft pillows, then I, perchance before they wish, shall arouse them from their slumbers by hammering on their doors at dawn'.[46] This tone fits better with Henry's stance in 1415 than in 1414, and also with French confidence arising out of the reconciliation between the Burgundians and Armagnacs at which the English ambassadors were present: a letter sent by Thierry Gherbode to Paris noted that 'the English ambassadors were not at all happy . . . this does not cause me concern but they have made it clear that they intended their plans to be fulfilled in France this summer', in other words, through an invasion.[47]

Whatever the date and form of the tennis-ball incident, it reflects Henry's poor international reputation in the early stages of his reign. The French did not take him seriously. Even in 1415 a Frenchman reported the view that he was overweight and often ill.[48]

Now, war was Henry's only option – which in any case seems increasingly to be what he wanted personally. Although the French sent a last-minute embassy to England in June, when Henry had moved to Winchester in preparation for departure, it was largely for show – to ensure that Henry was painted as the obvious aggressor – as well as to check on the effectiveness of Henry's mobilization. Henry responded to the French attempt to seize the moral high ground by having copies made of the offers of the Armagnac lords in 1412 for the restoration of the Brétigny lands, which he sent to the Council of Constance and to its leading negotiator, Sigismund of Luxemburg, king of the Germans and subsequently emperor, 'that all Christendom might know what great acts of injustice the French in their duplicity had inflicted on him, and that, as it were reluctantly and against his will, he was being compelled to raise his standards against rebels'.[49]

Although Henry was able to raise men and money for his expedition, neither was easy. He wanted a twelve-month campaign of conquest, but he did not have enough cash in hand to pay soldiers' wages expected in advance, even with taxation income and loans from the city of London and other English towns and individuals as well as from Italian merchants, a group prominent in European credit mechanisms. Before the indentures (contracts for service) for the campaign were struck on 29 April, the Lords discussed the problem among themselves and told the king that he had to make a sufficient guarantee for payment beyond the first three months of service.[50] The solution was to give captains items from the royal jewel collection as surety for the second three months, with an obligation for the crown to find funds to redeem such items in January 1417. Although kings had used jewels and plate before to secure loans from corporations and individuals, and Henry had pawned his 'petits joyaulx' to support his troops in Wales when prince, 1415 is the first, and perhaps only, time when they were pledged directly to captains entering into indentures to serve on a military campaign.[51] The mechanism worked but Henry was essentially mortgaging the future and needed success in France to raise further taxation and loans in order to redeem the jewels.

There was anxiety in the royal council about ensuring that other commitments for the defence of the realm were not overlooked. 'Before the departure of the king adequate provision should be made,' reads one minute.[52] It was deemed essential to send a total of 1,800 troops to the marches of Scotland, Wales and Calais and for the defence of the Channel, and royal agents were even despatched into Wales in the hope of finding the still-uncaptured Owain Glyndŵr to come to a deal and thereby pre-empt any problems during the king's absence.[53] The supposed spy Jean Fusoris reported at his trial in France that 'a doctor' in the royal household had told him that a marriage would have been better for Henry than a war, and that there were many who favoured his brother Thomas or Edmund, Earl of March. If the king proceeded with his invasion, the doctor had added, there would be a rising against him in England while he was absent. If he launched a campaign into France but came back quickly with little to show for all the expense that had been incurred, he would not be well received on his return.[54]

In fact, the revolt against him came before his departure. The Southampton Plot, as it is known, involved Henry's cousin Richard, Earl of Cambridge and the Northumberland knight Sir Thomas Grey of Heton. What precisely they intended to do remains unclear – the documents giving their confessions are damaged – but it seems that discussions had been going on for a while. There was talk of bringing down from Scotland the man who claimed to be Richard II, linking this to a Scottish invasion as well as involvement of the Percys. There was also an idea of taking the Earl of March to Wales and stirring up revolt there in order to attack Henry. All of these echoed problems for the crown under Henry IV. Finally, there was the simple notion of killing the king and his brothers.

Two elements make the plot serious. The first was that it was intended to happen while the king was gathering troops for embarkation and therefore, on the face of it, well protected, unless the plotters anticipated that there were others who thought like them. They claimed in their confessions that they had support even of the Earl of Arundel and other lords. Perhaps there was not total support for Henry's invasion plans. The second element was that the plot involved men of status close to the king, especially his cousin Richard whom he had only recently elevated to an earldom. Henry, Lord Scrope, much trusted by the king as a negotiator with Burgundy in 1414 and treasurer during the prince's period of control of the council in 1410–11, also fell foul of the king for failing to disclose the plot. The Earl of March, influenced perhaps by the fact that Henry V had treated him honourably, chose to alert the king although he had done little to discourage the plotters earlier. Sir Thomas Grey claimed that Scrope had told the earl 'that you [i.e. the king] were undone whether you abode or went'.[55]

Henry acted swiftly, executing his cousin Richard, Grey and Scrope after a summary trial. The plot indicates that, despite Henry's efforts to establish his kingship, there were still areas of weakness, even close at home. It is interesting to note, also, how the first two Lancastrian kings tended to make enemies of their erstwhile friends. This happened twice for Henry, with Oldcastle and the Southampton plotters. Even if the threat of deposition had not been great, there had been a threat. That Henry dealt so quickly with the Southampton Plot, showing no mercy even to those who had served him well, helped to strengthen his position as he prepared to sail for France, although by terror rather than persuasion. By the time he left England on 11 August, his obsession with invading France, which he saw as his God-given mission, overruled all other sentiments. He could not lose face at home or abroad by aborting the expedition now.

3
Agincourt and Normandy

So seduced are we by the idea of Shakespeare's 'happy few' that the scale of Henry V's invasion of France tends to go unrecognized. Henry's expedition of 1415 was the first time since Edward III's of 1359 that an English king had led a force to France in person, and he was intent upon making a substantial showing. His army, approaching 12,000, was larger than that of 1359 and not much smaller than that of 1346 with which Edward III had gained his celebrated victory at Crécy. On that occasion, Edward had conducted a raid across Normandy but had made no permanent conquests. By contrast, Henry V was determined to take and occupy French territory. To that end, he engaged troops for the lengthy and costly period of twelve months, requiring them to provision themselves with a three months' supply of food, an indication that he envisaged the men being used in sieges rather than the destructive burning and pillaging of the *chevauchée*, in which living off the land was an essential part of strategy. Indeed, Henry also took a strong force of gunners, miners, masons and other support staff appropriate to siege warfare.

Henry's strategy was a new departure in English war policy and reveals an ambitious as well as an imaginative approach. Tenure of territory, especially the wealthy and economically important duchy of Normandy, offered the prospect of considerable financial benefit. At the parliament of November 1414, the chancellor had pointed out that 'if their prince had a greater increase in his patrimony, it would be possible to reduce the burdens on his subjects'.[1] Moreover, Henry may already have had in mind a distribution of conquered lands to his soldiers. Securing Norman ports would also remove the threats posed to English shipping: Harfleur, at the mouth of the Seine, had been a particular hotbed of the piracy condoned by the French government. Given the strong mercantile lobby in Parliament and in London, this strategy would be appealing at home. Furthermore, it was relatively easy to resupply and reinforce Normandy from England. Conquests would fortify Henry's negotiating position with the French as well as demonstrating on the European stage that the English were a force to be reckoned with.

Henry's presence in France would be an intolerable insult to the French, who would be bound to respond and bring him to battle, something which, given the size of his army, would be a considerable challenge as it would take the French both time and money to raise a force large enough to face him, thereby giving him time to establish his position by conquering territory. That said, if Henry had hoped to benefit from the legacy of tensions between the rival French factions, the Armagnacs and Burgundians, either by allying with one of them or expecting them to be weakened by their earlier divisions, then he would be disappointed. The reconciliation they had made on 23 February persisted.

The initial advantage lay with Henry as invader. The French could not raise an army quickly enough to bring to battle his large army during his siege of Harfleur (17 August–22 September 1415) and made no effort to do so. Yet the campaign did not go as planned. Harfleur proved more difficult to take than he had expected: the siege dragged on for five weeks. Henry had adopted a threatening tone, claiming his powers according to Chapter 20 of the Book of Deuteronomy to act savagely against the town and its inhabitants if it refused to surrender. Indeed, he is the first Western European king known to have explicitly cited this biblical precedent in war, which allowed rulers to act harshly against places which they considered to be theirs by right and which resisted their authority. He had first alluded to it in the final letter he had sent to Charles VI on 28 July before he launched his invasion.[2] The unnamed author of the *Gesta Henrici Quinti* ('Deeds of Henry the Fifth'), a priest accompanying Henry's army, tells us that as soon as he had come to the throne, the king had 'written out for himself the laws of Deuteronomy in his bosom',[3] suggesting this biblical awareness may have been linked to his religious transformation on accession. The townspeople decided to surrender when Henry threatened to launch an assault and when they discovered that the French king and his son were not able to relieve the siege because they could not raise a large enough army at this point.

Henry's strong belief that it was God who had given him the victory coloured the manner of his entry to Harfleur, barefoot and culminating with prayers and oblations at the Church of Saint-Martin. This did not disguise his intention to make the town a second Calais, expelling much of the population and encouraging English settlers with a promise of houses and even a charter of liberties. But the victory came at a cost. His army was too large to be kept in one confined location for so long and, thanks to the insanitary conditions, was stricken by dysentery. At least 1,330 had to be invalided home, with an unknown number dying at the siege. These included Henry's long-standing friend and adviser Richard Courtenay, who died at Harfleur on 15 September. Henry's devotion to him was such that his body was taken back to England for burial near to the king's own proposed tomb in Westminster Abbey. A second close friend, the Earl of Arundel, had been invalided home but died in England on 13 October; the king's brother Thomas had also returned home sick.

Harfleur's defences had been so badly damaged by English bombardment that Henry had to install an exceptionally large garrison of 1,200 men under Thomas Beaufort, Earl of Dorset, to ensure that the French would not be tempted into an early attempt at recovery. With perhaps a third of his men no longer free to continue the campaign, and with autumn drawing on, Henry abandoned efforts to progress deeper into France and decided to withdraw to the English port of Calais. While making preparations to do so, he sought both to test and insult the French by summoning the dauphin, Louis, to personal combat, the winner to succeed Charles VI at his death.[4] He did this just to show that he had the upper hand as he knew it would generate no response.

Although Henry's campaign had demonstrated the English

ability to invade and damage France, his conquests had not been as extensive or achieved as quickly as he had hoped. By withdrawing now he could limit the financial burden, enabling him to recover more easily the jewels and plate distributed to his captains as security for the wages of the second three-month period of service. Not confident of making further conquests at this stage, he was keen to minimize risks in the hope of coming back to France in a stronger position later. By moving away from Harfleur towards Calais, which he did between 6 and 8 October, it was less likely that the French would make an immediate attempt to retake Harfleur. Rather, they would be tempted to pursue Henry as he made his way northwards.

He did not wish to face the French in battle at this point. His initial route close to the coast of Upper Normandy shows that he wanted to get to Calais as quickly as possible: the author of the *Gesta* anticipated that the march north would take eight days once the army had set out from Harfleur.[5] But, having arrived at the mouth of the Somme, Henry learned that the French had assembled a large army on the north bank of the estuary, thereby blocking his route to Calais. Knowing how vulnerable his army would be if intercepted during or immediately after crossing a wide river, since it could not easily be put into battle formation, Henry moved eastwards along the south bank of the Somme to seek a safer crossing. The *Gesta* portrays his eventual crossing of the river on 19 October over sixty miles inland as a major military achievement, one that was likely to enable Henry to avoid an engagement: 'we were of the firm hope that the enemy army ... would be disinclined to follow after us to do battle'.[6] The crossing put the onus on the French to intercept him before he reached Calais. Thus, on 20 October, the French commanders, already gathering their forces at Péronne, sent heralds to Henry to tell him that they would do battle with him before he reached the town. It is possible that they had chosen Aubigny as the battle location at this point, but since Henry deliberately moved off in a different direction, still trying to avoid battle, the French ended up intercepting him close to Agincourt (the present-day village of Azincourt), thirty-four miles south of Calais as the crow flies.

At first sight, advantages in a pitched battle lay with the French. Henry's army had been reduced in size to about 8,500 and had a preponderance of archers, over 80 per cent of the total force, who were not fully armed and therefore vulnerable in the face of a cavalry charge. Some of the French army had shadowed Henry's march and even before he crossed the Somme he was anticipating being brought to battle. At Corbie on 17 October, he had ordered his archers to provide themselves with six-foot-long stakes sharpened at each end to place in the ground in front of them to protect them against the expected French cavalry attack. We must assume that he, or others in his company, had heard of the effectiveness of stakes at Nicopolis in 1396 in protecting the Ottoman forces and thereby contributing to their victory against the allied crusader forces. Throughout the march he also imposed strict discipline on his troops, even making soldiers who found wine at one of the castles en route empty out the bottles they had filled.

Henry's leadership did much to keep up English spirits.

This was particularly valuable when the English arrived at Agincourt on 24 October and saw a large French host blocking their route. He expected battle to be given that day. Drawing up his troops, he 'very calmly and quite heedless of danger, gave encouragement to his army'.[7] In fact, the French chose not to engage. A delay suited them since it would increase English anxiety as well as allow for their late-comers to arrive. As it transpired, not all did come in time to fight. The Duke of Brittany, for instance, was still at Amiens on 25 October, and although the Duke of Brabant did reach Agincourt, it was not until most of the battle was over.

The French did not have as large an army as they had hoped. Knowing exactly how many they had is problematic but the numbers could not have been nearly as high as the often ridiculously inflated figures given in the chronicles. A tax to support 6,000 men-at-arms and 3,000 *gens de trait* (crossbowmen as well as longbowmen) had been levied, and we can add in others raised by the *semonce des nobles* (a summons to the nobility and those 'accustomed to follow the wars' to provide service, although usually still in expectation of pay), from Normandy and Picardy (according to the chroniclers' lists of dead, most of the slain came from these areas) as well as troops from the north-eastern borders. A total around 12,000 is not unrealistic, and still considerably more than the 8,500 or so in Henry's army. But while the English benefited from the fact they had been together for over two months under a king who had grown into a strong and charismatic leader, and had had time to work out tactics, the French army had come together in dribs and drabs. It had been decided that Charles VI and

And ther ben othyr bestis .v. of chase
The buk the first the do the secûde
The fox the thryde which ofte hap hard grace
The ferthe the martyn & ye last the cõo
And sothe to say ther be no mo of tho
And cause why yt men shulde the more be sur
They shewen here also in portreture
And cause why they be set in portretur
Is this like as lecture put thyng in mende
Of lerned men ryght so a peyntyde fygure
Remembryth men vnlernyd in hys kende
And in ewrythyng for sothe the same I fynde
Therfore sith lerned may seme in ye book
The ymages shal ye lewd if he wole look

1. Edward, Duke of York dedicated his *Master of the Game*, a
translation into English of the *Livre de chasse* by the great huntsman
Gaston Fébus, Count of Foix, to his cousin, Prince Henry.

2. At the top of this Gloria can be seen 'le roy Henry' (King Henry). The composer is thought to be Henry V or else his father, Henry IV.

hed w dupnkes and oder cures but thes myght not
and at the laste the sayd John Bradmore enpri
metpnes of ys sayd cuf and had owt ys arow
hede wyth slevche an Instrumet ys wyche
Instrumet
was madi
the man of tonges and was Rolund and
holowyche be the myddf ther of entryd
a bybyll wyse w ys wyche Instrumet was
pullyd owt ys appolt hed and aft ward ys wound
was wasched w wyns and clensyd w wndrsica
tyfs onpmet of iij partf of popnlion and ys
iiij part of bony so contnewyngs ys space of
by dayes and aftward ys place was w
Jon Enson cyrurgyen And wndrstond for

3. John Bradmore, the surgeon who successfully removed an arrow
from Prince Henry's cheek after the Battle of Shrewsbury in July
1403, helpfully drew the instrument he devised for the purpose.

ve and noble prince excellent
My lord the prince my lord gracious
I humble servant and obedient
Unto your estate hye and glorious
Of which I am full tender and full zelous
Me recommande unto your worthynesse
With hert entier and spirite of mekenesse

4. Thomas Hoccleve wrote *The Regiment of Princes* in
1410–11 during Henry's period of prominence in his father's
government. In this manuscript copy from the 1430s Hoccleve
is portrayed presenting his work to the prince.

Il guerran dit   contes deu et de riche
vcy comment   et plusieurs autres b
par ung beu   capitaines le conte

5. This imagined scene of the Battle of Agincourt is taken from a
copy made in the 1470s of the chronicle of Enguerran de Monstrelet.

6. A detail from Henry V's Great Bible. In the will Henry made before setting out to France in 1421, he bequeathed his Great Bible, which he had inherited from his father, to his own, as yet unborn, successor.

7. Even though Henry was in France in 1418/19 when he wrote this letter, he was still concerned with events in England. Here he orders that close guard be kept on the Duke of Orléans, captured at Agincourt.

8. The fourteenth-century keep of the castle of Vincennes, lying to the east of Paris, was where Henry V died on 31 August 1422.

9. This portrait of Henry V was painted in England by an unknown artist in the late sixteenth or early seventeenth century.

the dauphin would not participate (a sign that the French continued to be worried about Henry's potential strength). Therefore the leading commander was Charles, Duke of Orléans, with little military experience, who had been intruded at the last minute into an existing battle plan drawn up for an engagement closer to the Somme. Initially the Dukes of Burgundy and Orléans had both been told to keep away from the battle, the French crown being mindful of the long-running dispute between them.

On the morning of 25 October, both sides drew up their forces. The French placed in their vanguard a large proportion of their men-at-arms, perhaps as many as 5,000, intending to roll over by their sheer weight of numbers the small number of their English counterparts (who cannot have exceeded 1,500 men-at-arms) and to capture the king. The French had at least one further large division of men-at-arms, but it is not certain whether they had a third division at the rear. They were reluctant to deploy their crossbowmen and longbowmen, perhaps because they saw them as too few in number in comparison with the English missile-men and therefore vulnerable against the weight of English arrow power. Crossbows needed time for reloading and the soldier was exposed in the meantime. They decided to have the cavalry forces on each flank charge against the English archers to knock them out of the fight. This was a sensible move in principle but it did not work as planned. First, it seems that troops were reluctant to join the cavalry force since they preferred to fight in the vanguard, where the more valuable prisoner gains were likely to be made. Therefore the cavalry forces were not large enough to be effective. It may be also that the French who had been detailed to the cavalry charge against the archers realized the devastating effect arrows would have on horses, which were not usually well armoured, and preferred not to join the charge against the archers. Secondly, because Henry had protected his archers with stakes, this made it difficult for the charge to keep up the necessary momentum. Thrown into disarray, the horsemen turned to retreat, only to collide into their next ranks and into the vanguard of French men-at-arms advancing on foot.

Henry's success derived chiefly from his astute deployment of archers. With such a large number at his disposal, he placed them on the flanks as well as in front of his three divisions of men-at-arms. Protected by the stakes, they were able to keep up a veritable barrage of arrows against which the French cavalry and foot advance was impeded. The arrow storm created a frightening situation into which the French had no choice but to try to keep going. A natural funnelling effect ensued, with the advancing foot soldiers becoming so closely packed they could not even raise their weapon arms. Men fell and others fell on top of them. It appears also that the ground over which the French had to advance was muddy from the nature of the soil, newly sown crops and the overnight rain. Many died from suffocation or effectively drowned in the mud, never even reaching the English men-at-arms to engage with them.

Henry had been astute in his positioning, the result no doubt of scouting on the eve of battle. As head of the smaller army, he had adopted a defensive position even if he had had to make an initial move forward to a new position in order to goad the French into attack (another sign that they were still hoping for more reinforcements to arrive). He commanded the centre battle. All accounts emphasize his personal valour: his brother Humphrey fell but the king stood over him to protect him until he could be taken to safety. Henry participated fully in the fight, leading his troops by example. His cousin Edward, Duke of York commanded the vanguard, the English first division which bore the brunt of French attack, the duke thereby falling in action. The rearguard was under the command of Thomas, Lord Camoys, who had married into the fringes of the royal family, and who, as a seasoned sixty-five-year-old, was able to hold the line and confidence of his troops while they awaited the attack.

With their advance slowed, the French men-at-arms were an easy target for the English. Even the archers, despite their lack of weaponry, could climb on to the piled-up French and use whatever they had to hand – hammers, axes and daggers – to despatch men who under other circumstances would be too well armed for them to challenge at all. As a consequence, the later French divisions, seeing what was happening, simply left the field. In this context, the size of the French army was immaterial since by no means everyone took part. Henry considered the battle won, and stood down his army, ordering men to search through the heaps of French for prisoners. There was enough of a time lapse for prisoners to be rounded up. But at some point – we do not know exactly how much later – a shout went up that the French were intending to launch a new attack. This was probably the late arrival of the Duke of Brabant. Henry realized his army was in no position to respond. Men had taken off their helmets and gauntlets and were out of position. Therefore he ordered the prisoners to be killed. In the reminiscence of Ghillbert de Lannoy, who was in 1415 chamberlain to Philip, son of Duke John of Burgundy:

> I was wounded in the knee and head and lay with the dead. When the bodies were searched through I was taken prisoner . . . and kept under guard for a while. I was then led to a house nearby with 10 or 12 other prisoners who were all wounded. And there, when the duke of Brabant was making a new attack, a shout went up that everyone should kill his prisoners. So that this might be effected all the quicker, they set fire to the house where we were.[8]

Callous as this act appears to be (other sources suggest prisoners were killed by weapons too), Henry had been placed in a vulnerable position. To protect his own men, he had to act quickly and decisively. No contemporary source makes any criticism of his decision to kill the prisoners. All save one connect it to the real danger of a new French attack. (The exception is the chronicler Pierre Fenin's link to the attack on the English baggage train, an event which certainly took place but during the initial stages of the battle, leading to the loss, among other things, of some of the king's own possessions.) It was fully accepted that no commander could endanger his own side: French and Castilian prisoners were ordered by the Portuguese commanders to be killed during the Battle of Aljubarrota in 1385 when it was believed that a new attack was imminent. Nor could Henry allow a victory which he had already won to be taken from him. This also explains why he moved away from the battlefield quickly on the following day, and maintained a defensive position on his march to Calais, which he reached on 29 October.

For many today, the Battle of Agincourt stands as Henry's main achievement. Yet it was hardly a decisive victory in the way Poitiers (1356) had been, since that had seen the capture of the King of France, thereby requiring the French to negotiate his release and to agree to a treaty which gave Edward III substantial territory in France. Neither Charles VI nor the dauphin was present at Agincourt, and the prisoners were not so politically important that they would force the French to the negotiating table. Agincourt resembled Crécy in that respect. Like Crécy, too, there were very low rates of mortality on the English side and large numbers on the French, a situation which made the French reluctant ever to meet the English in battle again. Unlike Crécy, however, Agincourt saw large numbers of French captives – even after the killing of the prisoners – which offered potential profit to the crown as well as its soldiers. At least 320 prisoners are known, with an authenticated figure of around 500 dead. This contrasts with estimates of English dead, which some sources place as lower than 30 but which probably exceeded 100. Even so, the extent of victory is revealed by the asymmetric effects of the battle on the armies. Henry's victory redeemed what might otherwise have been a disappointing campaign for the English. Battles were relatively scarce, and ones on this scale involving a crowned head even rarer. But the political advantage for Henry in England was immense and perhaps the greatest impact of the battle. It secured his position once and for all, and he did much to exploit the victory to enhance his kingship.

He may initially have contemplated continuing the campaign. That was the impression he wanted to give to the parliament which opened on 4 November 1415 while he was still absent in France. The chancellor's opening speech reported his successes at Harfleur and Agincourt – 'praise be to God, with the greatest honour and gain which the realm has ever had in so short a time' – but warned that without further financial assistance this 'propitious, honourable and profitable expedition' could not continue. The Lords and Commons were invited to consider 'how provision could be made in this matter . . . such as will be suitable for the completion and continuation of the expedition'.[9] Whether Henry really was considering prolonging the campaign, perhaps with an attack on the Burgundian-held stronghold of Ardres on the edge of the Calais march, seems unlikely: if so, he appears to have been dissuaded by his leading captains. More likely, the king was worried about his financial resources more generally, and felt that Parliament would be more likely to vote him another tax if it believed he wanted to continue in arms. And so it turned out: after the instalment of the lay subsidy scheduled for payment in February 1416 had been brought forward to December 1415, a new subsidy had been granted for November 1416 and the king had been awarded the trade taxes for life, he announced the campaign completed and brought his army home. Parliament closed on 13 November. Three days later, Henry landed in England.

On 23 November he entered London in triumph, with the citizens arranging and paying for a series of tableaux in his honour and also theirs, to emphasize the status of the city itself and their own prestige. At the end of London Bridge the giants Gog and Magog, traditional guardians of the city, were dressed in all their finery, 'bent upon seeing the eagerly awaited face of their lord and welcoming him with abundant praise'.[10] En route the king was greeted by choirs and heraldic displays. The tower of the water conduit at Cornhill was covered with crimson cloth and decorated with the royal arms as well as those of St George, St Edward the Confessor and St Edmund. As the king passed it, 'a company of prophets' with white hair, golden copes and turbans released, 'as an acceptable sacrifice to God for the victory', sparrows and other small birds. 'Some descended onto the king's breast, some settled upon his shoulders, and some circled around in twisting flight', while the prophets chanted 'sing to the Lord a new song, Alleluia'.[11] At the Cheapside cross, a choir of beautiful young maidens adorned in white, 'sang "Welcom Henry ye fifte, Kynge of Englon and of Fraunce" as if to another David coming from the slaying of Goliath, who might appropriately be represented by the arrogant French'.[12] This was not a Roman-style triumph, however. The king was accompanied not by his whole army but by a small retinue, and only the six most important prisoners were paraded. Onlookers were struck by the king's humble demeanour, which underlined his constant emphasis on the God-given nature of his victory. The procession culminated in religious devotion at Westminster Abbey.

All mention of Agincourt after the event was consciously linked to God's support for the king. The idea of God-given victory was not new, but Henry pushed it to new heights as part of his vision of kingship. It was also fanned by his advisers – at least one of whom, notwithstanding the king's self-conscious projection of humility, was worried that the victory would go to the king's head:

> Thy royal majesty deems and firmly holds, as I presume, that not thy hand, but the outstretched hand of God, hath done all these things, for His own praise, the honour and glory of the English nation, and the eternal memory of the royal name ... Moreover, it is fitting that your royal highness should not boast of the past, but be anxious for the future; neither let the power of our enemies drag us back; let not their astuteness disturb us; nor let any fair promises seduce any one.[13]

The author of these words was, very probably, Henry's uncle and chancellor, Henry Beaufort: if so, they were perhaps written with Henry's behaviour as prince, as well as king, in mind.

But if the implication of these words was that Agincourt provided a decisive advantage in terms of Anglo-French politics, it did not prove to be the case. Indeed, rather than respond to the crushing defeat with diplomatic efforts to come to terms, the French aimed to strike back as fast as possible, with an attempt to recover Harfleur. The English conquest was proving very difficult to sustain, especially in terms of supplying food to the garrison there; indeed, increasingly desperate sorties in March 1416 had ended in near disaster, with losses of both men and horses. By early April, the French had laid a naval blockade against the town and had established garrisons on the landward side. The Earl of Dorset, who had been appointed captain of Harfleur at its surrender, was at the end of his tether by the middle of the month. He had written to the royal council on several occasions for food, artillery and other items, 'but,' he noted in a strongly worded despatch, 'nothing has been provided', which was 'extremely disappointing to myself and the loyal subjects of the king ... if meat is not sent as soon as possible we will have to return home at Whitsun' (7 June).[14]

Since late January that year, Henry had been drawing up plans to lead another expedition to France.[15] But while Parliament, sitting again throughout March and April 1416, agreed to bring forward to June the subsidy due for payment in November, the problem of Harfleur forced Henry on to the defensive. In late May and early June, an army of 7,500 was raised to save Harfleur, its ratio of one man-at-arms to two archers, as opposed to the one to three preferred for land campaigns, reflecting the intention to use it at sea, where longbowmen were not needed in large numbers.

But although Henry had moved to the Southampton area in early July, he did not participate in the naval campaign that followed, which was under the command of his brother John, Duke of Bedford. Two months earlier, Henry had welcomed Sigismund of Luxemburg, the king of the Germans, whom the English already called emperor, who had arrived in England keen to broker peace between England and France for the sake of a solution at the Council of Constance to the papal schism. Sigismund's visit was a diplomatic coup for Henry – European rulers rarely deigned to cross the Channel – and he responded in kind, spending lavishly on entertaining his imperial visitor and, on 24 May, investing him with the Order of the Garter. It was, apparently, Sigismund who persuaded Henry that it was too dangerous for him, and potentially harmful to the common good, 'for the king to risk the perils of the sea in person'.[16]

At the end of May, Sigismund was joined in England by William, Count of Holland, Zealand and Hainault, with the idea that both should try to broker a settlement between England and France. But their solution – that Harfleur should be placed in the emperor's hands – was acceptable neither to Henry (who had added it to the gains made by Edward III at the Treaty of Brétigny in 1360 as essential to any peace) or the French, who assumed they would soon retake the town. Accepting failure, Sigismund was willing to enter into a perpetual alliance with Henry, which was sealed at Canterbury on 15 August – the very same day, as chance would have it, that the navy led by his brother John, Duke of Bedford routed the French at the Battle of the Seine, and saved Harfleur for the English.

The Treaty of Canterbury recognized Henry's rights against the French and in theory offered imperial support in their implementation – although, as it transpired, the emperor never would give military aid to Henry. But the treaty was significant simply in its signing. Here was evidence that Henry, based on his successes against the French, was now seen as a serious player in Europe. Equally significant was a meeting brokered by Count William, to take place at Calais the following October, between Henry and William's brother-in-law, John the Fearless, Duke of Burgundy.

What both parties hoped to get out of this meeting, and what exactly happened at it, remains shrouded in mystery. According to one undated English diplomatic source, Duke John was inclined to support Henry's claim to the French crown; another, however, reports that, when offered by Henry a share in any future French conquests, the duke refused.[17] It is unlikely that any understanding between Henry and Duke John was reached. Furthermore, Burgundian power in France was uncertain at this point since the duke had neither a formal role in government nor any control of the king. Indeed, his purpose in agreeing to a meeting with the English king was simply to remind his internal enemies in France, the Armagnac party, that he could stir up trouble if he felt so inclined.

That autumn it soon became apparent that Henry was bent on a new land campaign in France, with or without Burgundian aid. Although his victories had made the winning of support at home easier, it was by no means guaranteed: Henry still had to engage in the politics of persuasion. At the parliament which began at Westminster on 19 October 1416, Chancellor Henry Beaufort's opening speech emphasized not only the king's martial successes in France in 1415 but also his efforts at the Leicester parliament of 1414 to have law observed within the realm. The speech included the call 'let us make wars so that we might have peace, for the end of war is peace'.[18] A war, therefore, represented firm kingship towards achieving 'justice' at home and abroad. In this, Beaufort reflected how Henry wanted to portray himself: as a just and peaceful king. Keen as he was to go to war, he was equally anxious to be seen to avoid shedding Christian blood. Here, then, war was portrayed not as an end in itself but as a way of bringing – or, more accurately, forcing – the French to peace. This would, it was implied, be a long campaign, but confidence in a positive outcome was encouraged by a biblical analogy. Reference was made to the fact that this was the king's sixth parliament. As with the Creation, which came to full fruition on the seventh day, a perfect and early completion was surely at hand.

The Commons were persuaded, and granted a double lay subsidy, worth £76,000, three-quarters of which they generously agreed could be collected by February 1417. Such an arrangement gave Henry much more cash in hand than he had had for his campaign of 1415, two years before, and allowed him to begin raising troops as soon as the money started coming in. But another decision at the parliament also reveals that there had been some reservations about the credit mechanisms Henry had used for mobilizing troops in 1415. Although it was agreed that current tax income could be used as security for loans, the king had to promise to work hard to repay them; his brothers Thomas and John were also placed under obligation to do this should the king die in the meantime.

Here, Henry revealed himself as a skilled negotiator, willing to compromise in order to achieve his desired outcome, something also seen in his efforts to deal with other financial issues still outstanding from 1415 concerning his use of jewels for the wages of the second quarter of service. The indentures for the Agincourt campaign had committed Henry to redeem the pawned royal jewels within nineteen months – that is, by January 1417, which was now only a couple of months away. Meanwhile, on 19 November 1416, the day after Parliament ended, a list of those who fought at Agincourt was delivered by Sir Robert Babthorpe, controller of the king's household, to the Exchequer. This surely reflects the views of the nobility that, before indentures for a new campaign were drawn up, the crown needed to settle its Agincourt debts: many of Henry's captains had ended up paying soldiers from their own pockets.

The king was also asked to answer other unresolved matters. These concerns, in fact, are revealed by a set of council minutes for 6 March 1417, in which both the questions and the king's answers are noted. The fifth question posed to Henry concerns 'whether those accounting for men killed at the battle of Agincourt should have allowed to them the whole of the second quarter or only to the day of their death'. Henry replied that 'they should be allowed as the others who are now living'.[19] In other words, anyone killed at Agincourt was – like the survivors – to be deemed eligible to receive pay for the whole campaign. Therefore there was no need to record the Agincourt dead in the post-campaign accounting process, and it is why we have an incomplete knowledge of English fatalities. Henry's was a generous gesture, one useful for a king to make when on the point of recruiting a new army, and one which would also help to renew in people's minds the glory of the victory of 1415.

At the end of the parliament, Thomas Beaufort, who had defended Harfleur so vigorously in the aftermath of its conquest, was promoted from Earl of Dorset to Duke of Exeter: a reminder to the nobility and gentry, if one was needed, of the potential rewards for military service. An aggressively anti-French tone was also present in Parliament's confirmation of Henry's alliance with Sigismund, which, although an 'act of love' on the part of the emperor, none the less showed the French in a bad light and encouraged both the English as well as Sigismund's subjects to take up arms against them.[20] With the country gearing up for war, Henry granted a petition of the Fletchers of the City of London that clog makers should no longer be permitted to use aspen, since the timber was needed to make arrows, but only on the proviso that 'fletchers throughout the realm sell their arrows at a more moderate and reasonable price in future than they had sold them for previously'. Henry wanted to prevent producers exploiting what was obviously going to be increased demand for armaments as he prepared for his next campaign in France.[21] Meanwhile, both convocations of clergy, in the province of York as well as Canterbury, were equally generous in their tax grants. As a result, more money poured into the Exchequer in 1416–17 than at any other period between 1399 and 1485.

In the following months, Henry drew heavily on the glorious memory of Agincourt to ramp up public support for the forthcoming campaign. At his behest and with the support of the Archbishop of Canterbury, Henry Chichele, the Canterbury convocation agreed in December 1416 to a broad programme of commemoration for 25 October in the years to come. In the Canterbury province, prayers were to be shared on that day between Crispin and Crispinian, whose feast it was, St John of Beverley (whose feast of translation, when his body had been moved to a new shrine, was on the same day) and other martyrs. In contrast to the elevation in January 1416 of the feast of St George to the status of a double religious feast, where there was no mention of the battle, the wording of the December 1416 order invoked the battle explicitly: 'the gracious victory granted by the mercy of God to the English on the feast of the translation of the saint (St John of Beverley) to the praise of the divine name and to the honour of the kingdom of England'.[22]

Meanwhile, from February 1417 onwards, Henry set about mobilizing an army of over 10,000 men, only slightly smaller than his invasion force of 1415 but with similar proportions of men-at-arms and archers, with departure arranged for late July. Henry deliberately chose the date of his landing as 1 August, the feast of St Peter ad Vincula (St Peter in Chains), the notion being that, just as the apostle Peter was freed by an angel from King Herod's captivity, so Henry was liberating the Normans from the shackles of French rule. He was undertaking not simply a campaign of conquest but also a highly orchestrated recreation of the English duchy of Normandy, with the King of England as its duke. There had been elements of this in 1415, but nothing to compare with the comprehensiveness of the 1417 programme.

The duchy had been in the hands of the French crown for over two hundred years, ever since King John had lost it in 1204. In 1259, Henry III had acknowledged its surrender, dropping the title 'Duke of Normandy' which English kings had held since 1066. Now, in 1417, Henry's programme stressed two things. One was an appeal to Norman separatism. Despite the long tenure by the King of France, the duchy's inhabitants remained suspicious of the power of a distant Paris, sentiments that Henry was keen to exploit to his own advantage, offering the Normans their rights and privileges so long as they accepted his rule.

The second, complementary, aspect of his Norman policy was a deliberate invocation of the Anglo-Norman past, reinforcing Normandy's sense of separatism from France, and appealing to an English public. A crucial element was the granting of lands in Normandy to his soldiers and administrators as a kind of Norman Conquest in reverse. This policy, termed by historians the 'Lancastrian land settlement', persisted to the 1440s, throughout the English tenure of the duchy. Henry saw it as a way of generating a sense of investment in his war aims: those to whom lands were given were obliged to defend them, much as grantees in Ireland, Wales and Scotland had been in earlier generations. The terms of grants often involved service in defence of royal castles, as well as in the royal army, at the grantee's own expense. The settlement thus gave the king military resources, thereby reducing the burden on English finances. It also gave him substantial means of reward and patronage, suitable for all ranks of the army, ranging from a house in one of the captured towns for an archer and a whole county with its title for a high-ranking nobleman. In essence, Henry recreated 'feudalism' in Normandy. He used it to supplement the royal rights in France which he took over by virtue of his claim to the throne, especially the *semonce des nobles*, deploying it not only to call out the native nobility but also those to whom he had given lands.

An essential part of Henry's programme was a financial administration for the duchy through the establishment of a *chambre des comptes* (chamber of accounts) at Caen, his administrative capital, so that revenues came to him rather than to the French king in Paris. In time, as the conquest was secured, it was envisaged that the Estates of Normandy – an assembly made up of representatives of clergy, nobility and townsmen – could be called and taxation raised, in the hope that Henry's duchy would be self-financing. Although a separate Chancery enrolment (the Norman rolls) was initiated for the conquest, Henry was also keen to take over the existing administrative structures of the duchy such as the *bailliages* – administrative subdivisions under the French equivalent of sheriffs. He would appoint trusted Englishmen as *baillis*, but shrewdly ensured that lower-ranking officials, such as the *vicomtes*, were local men – with local knowledge – who had accepted English rule.

In order to implement this impressive political programme, Henry first needed a successful military campaign. It began on 1 August 1417, his entire army landing at the mouth of the River Touques in Lower Normandy: as in

1415, Henry initially kept his army together to besiege Caen but, in contrast with his first campaign, he also took care to establish smaller bridgeheads along the coast first. The capture of Caen took only two weeks, thanks largely to bombardment and the townspeople's early recognition that further resistance would only be to their disadvantage when there was no chance of a French army relieving the siege. With Caen taken, Henry was able to march directly south, capturing places as he went, thereby cutting Lower Normandy in half. Such quick and impressive success persuaded Parliament, meeting in mid November 1417, to agree another double lay subsidy: remarkable generosity given that they had made a similar award the previous year. As the chancellor put it: 'the king's great merits and illustrious virtues meant that he fully deserved such splendid honours'.[23]

By 24 November – indeed, probably from the moment of his landing – Henry styled himself Duke of Normandy as well as King of France. His generally conciliatory policy towards his conquered people, supported by strict discipline over his troops, was aimed at encouraging local acceptance. Only where Henry met with resistance did he act harshly. As a result, relatively few Norman knights and gentry chose exile rather than submission.

With the fall of Falaise at the turn of the year, Henry was able to divide his army under the command of his brothers Thomas and Humphrey, so that the areas to the east and west could be taken simultaneously. On 30 July 1418, with Lower Normandy in his hands, he began the siege of Rouen. This was the campaign's most formidable challenge to date for, as Henry noted in a letter to the city of London on

10 August, it was 'the most notable place in France save Paris'.[24] Well aware of the significance of the city militarily and politically, Henry was prepared to use any means to take it without extensive bombardment or assault, but in doing so, he also risked giving the French time to organize a counter-offensive to relieve the city. Determined to starve the city out, he refused to let even women and children leave.

The siege of Rouen lasted six months and when, in January 1419, it finally surrendered – the anticipated French relief force having been scuppered by a renewed outbreak of factional infighting – was the largest city ever to be taken by siege during the whole of the Hundred Years War. Henry appeared in the robes of the Duke of Normandy in the Norman capital, where he made various edicts in that guise to an assembly of Norman knights and townsmen, and also placed a high collective ransom on the city.

With the surrender of Rouen, the rest of Upper Normandy fell with little resistance. Save for the island of Mont-Saint-Michel, which never fell to the English, Henry was master of the whole duchy, able to implement all the elements of his Norman programme. His 1417–19 campaign was remarkable, testimony to his ever-increasing capacity as commander as well as ruler. Normandy would always mean something special to Henry: when he came to a final treaty with the French at Troyes in May 1420, he kept the duchy for himself until such time as he would inherit the French crown. That he had achieved a high level of success in winning the hearts and minds of the Normans is also indicated by the outpouring of grief at his death, and the loyalty they showed to his successors. Key to this was the strict military discipline he imposed, particularly in regulating relations between soldiers and civilians, and creating mechanisms for local inhabitants to lodge complaints. He took a notably hard line with camp followers, reflecting his own moral transformation on accession.

There is strong evidence that Henry was prepared in the summer of 1419 to agree a diplomatic settlement which would give him Normandy as a completely sovereign possession, without any obligation to pay homage to the French crown for it. That summer, his successes prompted approaches from both French factions, the Burgundians and the Armagnacs. In the face of Henry's advance, the French had maintained a united front until the summer of 1418, when the Burgundian duke John the Fearless seized Paris as well as the king and queen, forcing the then dauphin, Charles, to flee south – divisions that contributed to the failure of the French to intervene to rescue Rouen. Now, Henry was keen to negotiate with both parties – the Burgundian-controlled royal government as well as the Armagnac opposition, led by the dauphin – because he saw this as a means of keeping them divided, and ruling. His biggest concern was their reconciliation: a united France remained a formidable enemy.

Negotiations with the dauphin came first, at Alençon in October 1418. Henry, as he always had, set his demands high, now adding Normandy, Touraine and Maine to the lands stipulated in the Treaty of Brétigny, and even including Flanders as a reward for an alliance against Burgundy.[25] The dauphin was willing to give him Normandy – which in Henry's view was an empty gesture since God had already delivered it into his hands. None the less, he was willing to consider a long truce, during which he would drop the title of King of France in return for a large payment.

The following month saw negotiations at Pont-de-l'Arche with the Burgundian-controlled royal government. Henry demanded the Brétigny terms plus Normandy in full sovereignty, as well as a dowry of 1 million *écus* for marriage to Charles VI's daughter Catherine, whose hand in marriage he had requested four years before. Then, he had been rebuffed. Now, the situation was rather different. Henry, fully aware of his strong military position, was simply playing with his enemy. The continuing mental illness of Charles VI made it unclear whether anyone in the French camp had the authority to negotiate a settlement. In the words of the chronicler Jean Le Fèvre, the French 'were unable to treat with Henry, the dauphin is not yet king, and the duke of Burgundy does not possess the royal inheritance'.[26]

While the negotiations stalled, over the course of the spring of 1419 Henry strengthened his position in Normandy, conquering places on its northern frontier, which provided a buffer zone (called by the English the *pays de conquête*) against Paris. When, between late May and June, he met again with the Burgundian-controlled government at Meulan, they were prepared to offer the Brétigny terms plus Normandy and his dowry demands. Significantly, the eighteen-year-old Princess Catherine was brought to Meulan, where Henry saw her for the first time. Even without injecting a romantic element into Henry's chaste military existence, it was clear that the king was keen to marry, and to marry only Catherine: indeed, this had been the most consistent element in all of his negotiations from 1413 onwards. The meeting also brought him into direct contact with Charles VI and his queen, Isabeau of Bavaria, for the first time since they had all attended the wedding of Richard II to Catherine's sister Isabella near Calais nearly a quarter-century before.

The negotiations at Meulan are well documented, even to detailing how a special terrain was selected and demarcated by wooden palisades, and divided by two trenches into three parts.[27] The French would be located in the area nearest to Meulan and the English in the part furthest away; the middle section would be a neutral zone, where the negotiators met. The French, moreover, had a solid fence built around the middle section, high enough to protect against English arrows should things get nasty. This middle section was accessible only by three fenced passages and contained two separate tents at each side, one for each monarch and his counsellors. Exactly thirty-six feet from each tent, and within a further palisade, was the pavilion for actual negotiations.

Such elaborate arrangements, as well as the double royal presence, highlight the serious intent of both parties. That Catherine was there, too, indicates that a betrothal was the anticipated outcome. The fact that the negotiations covered detailed matters, including the restoration of lands and benefices in Normandy to those who supported the Burgundian regime, also suggests that a settlement was in sight. A letter sent home by an Englishman on 14 July reported that Henry had been hoping that the French would fulfil their promise that he and his heirs would have 'all that was contained in the Great Peace [Brétigny] ... the duchy of Normandy hool [whole] and all that the kynge had goten on the Frensh ground, to holde all thise things of God only and nat of noon Erthly creature'. But then, the writer continued, just when the negotiations were on the brink of being concluded and treaties drawn up, they had hit a brick wall. Suddenly, the accommodating behaviour of the French changed to obfuscation. In the words of the English writer, 'the French partie hath comen with diverses demandes and questions'. As these were fully intended to do, they caused delays, and the atmosphere had, accordingly, deteriorated: 'now at this tyme it is nat knowen whethir we shal have werre or pees'.

As the writer went on to tell his recipient in England, John the Fearless and the dauphin had been holding their own convention at Paris in the meantime. The duke, present for some of the time at Meulan, had been playing a double game, and as the writer explained, 'They have sette hem tweyne [together] in reste and in accord.' Their agreement had been proclaimed in Paris on 11 July, promising to work together to drive out the English, with orders that no one should henceforth make quarrel because of the name of Burgundian or Armagnac, 'for which accord it is supposed in the Kynges host rather werre than pees'.[28] It was precisely the outcome that Henry did not want.

Despite Henry's strength, as the letter writer had noted, the newly unified French were more interested in war than a negotiated settlement. Henry's hand was forced: without hesitation, he advanced towards Paris.

Taking the towns of Pontoise and Gisors, he was at the outskirts of Paris by mid August, when his brother Thomas, at Henry's order, rode up to the gates of Paris, a dramatic gesture intended to put pressure on the French towards reopening diplomatic channels. Whether Henry could realistically have seized the French capital is doubtful. Rouen had taken him six months, and now he had considerably fewer troops with him, having installed garrisons to secure his recent conquests en route to Paris. Furthermore, while the French had been divided during the siege of Rouen, now they threatened unity.

But before Henry needed to make up his mind whether to lay siege to Paris, the French tore themselves apart, in a way which gave the English king more success in France than he could ever have imagined. On 10 September 1419, Duke John and the dauphin were due to meet on the bridge at the town of Montereau, on the Seine east of Paris, for further discussions on their co-operation. As the duke moved on to the bridge, one of the dauphin's henchmen struck him in the face with an axe, killing him instantly. The factional conflict had degenerated into a vendetta, Duke John murdered in revenge for his assassination of Louis, Duke of Orléans twelve years before. Whether the dauphin was personally complicit remains uncertain. Only sixteen, he was presumably easily influenced by those who had previously been in the service of the dukes of Orléans, and who had carried out the murder of Duke John at Montereau. Despite their attempted reconciliation in the face of the

English threat, 'the two factions were as far apart as they had ever been'.[29] Not without cause did a Carthusian friar, almost exactly a century later, show Francis I, King of France, the skull of John the Fearless, observing 'this is the hole through which the English entered France'.[30] That hole effectively made Henry V the ruler of France.

4
Heir and Regent of France

In the Cathedral of Troyes, on 21 May 1420, Henry V was acknowledged by Charles VI, King of France, as heir to the French crown. In the opening passage of the treaty sealed on that day, Charles noted how several previous treaties had been made between his predecessors and those of 'the most high prince and our very dear son, Henry, king of England and heir of France' but none had brought the 'fruit of peace so desired'. Mindful of 'how much damage and sorrow had been caused by the division of the kingdoms to this point, not only for the kingdoms but also for the church', Charles was now making peace with Henry (even if, in reality, it had been Henry who had called the tune in the preceding negotiations). The thirty-one main clauses which follow give the terms of this peace. Henry was not to hinder Charles's possession of the French crown while he lived, but at his death the crown of France was to remain perpetually with Henry and his heirs. From that point on, the two crowns were always to be held by the same person, even though the two kingdoms would retain their liberties, customs, usages and laws.

It was not the Treaty of Troyes which made Henry heir to France: he was already that by virtue of the long-standing claim of English kings to the French crown. The crucial importance of Troyes was that a French king was now on record as having formally acknowledged that claim. What was more, while retaining his crown, Charles effectively passed his rule immediately to Henry: 'because we are hindered in such a way that we cannot personally attend to the disposition of the business of our realm, the faculty and exercise of governing and ordering "la chose publique" [everything concerning the good of the kingdom and its people] shall be vested in our son Henry'.[1] Over the next few weeks, we see Henry dropping his title of King of France and replacing it with 'heir and regent of France'.

To understand such an amazing and unexpected settlement, we need to return to the events of the previous autumn. The murder of John the Fearless by the dauphin's supporters at the bridge of Montereau on 10 September 1419 removed all hope of French unity and forced the Burgundians to ally with Henry. At this point, the French king and queen remained at Troyes, where they had been placed by Duke John in order to keep them under his control; the new Duke of Burgundy, John's son Philip, was in Lille; while most of the royal council was still under the control of Burgundian officials in Paris. The citizens of Paris, always a pro-Burgundian and powerful lobby, were alarmed that the murder might embolden Henry to make an attack on the capital. On 19 September 1419, the royal council, with the support of Paris, approached Henry for a truce, and to discuss revenge for the murder. Henry's response, five days later, was to empower his ambassadors to negotiate a final peace. Three days later, they made a declaration to the royal

council which emphasized Henry's right to the French
throne but, in wording presumably intended to reassure
the French, stated that he had no intention that 'his French
crown, kingdom or people should be subject to his English
crown, or that the people of France should become or
be called "English"'.[2] Once again, he proposed marriage
to Catherine, and although the declaration did not explicitly mention that Charles would remain king for the rest of
his life, it promised that Henry would treat his prospective
royal in-laws with the honour they deserved.

Henry was undoubtedly the originator of the terms later
enshrined in the Treaty of Troyes. He realized that it was to
his advantage to stake his claim before the French government and the new Duke of Burgundy had time to develop
their own response to the murder of Duke John. When the
council at Paris responded by saying the declaration was
not what Henry had been asking for in July, the king
replied bluntly: 'things are different now'.[3] Over the following week he developed his plans further, proposing Charles
remain king until death. In a flurry of diplomatic activity
with Paris, Lille and Troyes, the full terms of a final peace
were negotiated. Duke Philip gave his agreement on
2 December. For him, revenge against the dauphin – hitherto
the unquestioned Valois heir to the crown of France – for
his father's murder was paramount: his adherence to
Henry's terms brought the promise of English military support. Meanwhile, Henry ordered a closer watch be kept on
Charles, Duke of Orléans, who had been a prisoner in England since his capture at Agincourt: after all, what Henry
was proposing was effectively the disinheritance of the

whole of the Valois dynasty, and the duke was the next male heir after the dauphin. Henry had Louis Robessart, a close associate since 1403, sent to Troyes to help persuade Charles and his wife, Queen Isabeau, to accept English terms. With Duke Philip joining the king and queen at Troyes on 23 March, the full treaty was agreed on 9 April 1420 between the English, headed by the Earl of Warwick, and the French.

Henry moved from Pontoise on 8 May to the Abbey of Saint-Denis, the necropolis of French kings, where he paid his obligations as heir, before arriving at Troyes. On the same day the treaty was sealed, Henry and Catherine were betrothed; they were married less than two weeks later, on 2 June. The treaty was announced immediately in France and its terms sent back to England to be proclaimed so that 'al oure peuple may have verray [true] knowledge thereof for their consolacion'.[4]

Negotiations had added many clauses to the basic terms in order to serve the various parties involved. For instance, although Henry promised that any further conquests he made would be for the benefit of the French crown, he kept Normandy under his personal control until he became king, at which point it would be reintegrated into France: he realized that he could not draw back immediately from his encouragement of the Norman separatism which had facilitated his conquest. But the Burgundians were to have restoration of lands he had taken from their supporters in the duchy. Charles and Isabeau were reassured that they would only have French servants. Catherine's dowry was to be paid from English revenues: Henry's keenness led him to dispense with a requirement for a French dowry until he died, at which point his widow was henceforward to have 20,000 francs per annum. The Burgundian desire for revenge against the dauphin was guaranteed by a ban on any party included in the treaty negotiating with 'Charles, who calls himself Dauphin', and by a commitment on Henry to 'labour with all his might, and as soon as can profitably be done, to put into our obedience all the . . . places and persons within our realm disobedient to us, and rebels . . . of the party commonly called that of the Dauphin or Armagnac'.[5]

Henry's idea of allowing Charles VI to remain king may have come to his mind much earlier in the reign. When after the fall of Harfleur in 1415 he summoned the dauphin, Louis, to personal combat, Henry proposed that the victor should succeed Charles at his death. Yet it is hard to believe that Henry ever dreamed that the prospect of his being accepted as Charles's heir would become a reality. He drove a hard bargain in 1420, but was astute enough to know that much more was to be gained by negotiation than by conquest. Only through formal recognition by a king of France did a king of England have any chance of his claim to the French crown being recognized and implemented.

Meanwhile, the people of France were to take an oath to observe the treaty, with allegiance to Henry

[as] governor and regent of the kingdom of France, to obey him in all matters concerning the government which is subject to the king of France, and, after the death of Charles, to continue as liegemen and true subjects of Henry king of

England and his heirs forever, to accept and obey the same as sovereign lord and true king of France without opposition, contradiction or difficulty, coming to his aid as soon as requested.[6]

As regent and heir, Henry had access to all of the resources of the French kingdom, and all that he did was in the name of Charles VI.

A couple of days after his wedding, accompanied by Charles VI, Catherine and Philip of Burgundy, Henry went to besiege the Burgundian city of Sens, then under the control of the dauphin. This was an essential step towards recovering the town of Montereau, which Henry did in short order on 1 July, and with it the body of Duke John for burial in the Burgundian capital of Dijon. The siege of Melun followed. On the Seine near Paris, the town had held out against Henry: according to the chronicler Enguerran de Monstrelet, the inhabitants' refusal to surrender led Henry to bring Charles VI to receive their surrender as 'leur naturel seigneur' ('their natural lord').[7] The Treaty of Troyes had not ended war. Rather, war had mutated, becoming a rather different conflict in which Henry and his troops, in the name of the French king, collaborated with the Burgundians in their conflict with the Armagnacs.

Inevitably, not all Frenchmen accepted the Treaty of Troyes. Although the dauphin had fled south, his supporters were prepared to fight for his interests: Melun did not surrender to Henry until 1 November. Only then was it possible for Charles and Henry to make a ceremonial entry to Paris on 1 December. The choice of Advent Sunday was deliberate and the delay also allowed ample time for the streets to be decorated and the population to be clad in red to symbolize their rejoicing. The event was orchestrated to provide a visual representation of the treaty terms. The kings entered the city side by side with Charles on the right as the anointed King of France.[8] When relics were presented for the kings to kiss, Charles motioned for Henry to go first, but the latter touched his cap and gestured that Charles should precede him. The kings then entered Notre-Dame side by side, paying their devotions at the high altar.

On the following day the two queens, Catherine and Isabeau, entered Paris and were greeted by English lords and Duke Philip of Burgundy. The fact that they entered later and after their royal husbands reflected not only the lower status of queens but also the careful handling by Henry to avoid any suggestion that France had come to him through his marriage. Henry was already heir when he married; indeed, part of the reason that Catherine's dowry was to be paid from English revenues was to remove any notion that she brought France with her as her dowry to her husband. The marriage, although mentioned in the Treaty of Troyes, was given neutrally and simply there as being 'for the benefit of peace'. (Later, back in England, this was emphasized at the banquet on 24 February 1421 following Catherine's coronation in Westminster Abbey as Queen of England – which Henry did not attend – by a *sotelte*, a table decoration, labelled 'par marriage pur, ce guerre ne dure': 'by pure marriage, war shall cease'.)[9] The treaty did not require the kings of the double monarchy to be Henry's heirs by Catherine or even the heirs of his body, but simply his heirs general. That was why, immediately behind him on his entry into Paris, walked the two eldest of his brothers, Thomas and John, the Dukes of Clarence and Bedford. Henry had ensured that all elements of his rights and of the future of the English-held double monarchy had been covered.

The Treaty of Troyes had already effectively disinherited the dauphin by not recognizing him in this title, since to do so was to undermine Henry's own claim to the French throne. His formal disinheritance came on 23 December 1420 by a *lit de justice* – a formal session – in the *parlement* of Paris, France's principal law court, following French legal form. Meanwhile, shortly after the entry into Paris, Duke Philip and a representative of his mother made formal complaint against the dauphin for his role in the murder of Duke John. His petition was heard by Charles VI and Henry sitting side by side on the same bench, with the preservation of French institutions, as stipulated in the Treaty of Troyes, symbolized by the Chancellor of France and the first president of the *parlement* sitting at Charles's feet. The king, through his chancellor, promised that with the advice of Henry, King of England, regent and heir of France, justice would be done. The dauphin was duly found guilty and declared disinherited and an outlaw.

Although Henry's time as regent of France was being dominated by military activity, his influence on French government was substantial, as might be expected from a monarch who took his responsibilities seriously, and in a situation where Charles VI continued to suffer from 'absences', as royal documents called the periods when his mental state deteriorated, which made his active involvement in government inconsistent and minimal. Henry even issued some royal letters in his own name as heir, although the majority were in the name of Charles VI 'by the advice and deliberation of our beloved heir and regent the King of England'.[10] When in Paris, Henry held councils in person, as he did on 3 June 1422, and we find him consulted by the *parlement* and other bodies. He was also responsible for making appointments, always being careful, save for the higher military commands in Paris (to which he appointed his brother Thomas and subsequently the Duke of Exeter), to use Frenchmen of the Burgundian persuasion. His influence in ecclesiastical appointments was as influential as in England: in December 1420, the chapter of Notre-Dame elected Jean Courtecuisse as Bishop of Paris, a choice opposed by both Henry and Duke Philip. Although the appointment was confirmed by the pope, Henry remained recalcitrant and his influence was decisive: Courtecuisse was eventually appointed by the pope on 12 June 1422 to the bishopric of Geneva instead.

On 6 December 1420, Henry was present alongside Charles at the meeting of the Estates General in Paris as it ratified the Treaty of Troyes, welcoming it as being 'to the honour and praise of God as well as the public good and benefit of this kingdom of France and all its subjects'.[11] At Henry's behest, the Estates also discussed taxation, the outcome of which was an ordinance granting Henry the fruits of various sales taxes and a *gabelle* (salt tax) for one year from 1 February 1421. Such income was intended for military action against the dauphin. Concern was expressed at the Estates about the state of the currency: Henry's reforms as regent, including re-coinings and limitations on tax exemptions, did much to reverse the depreciation of the French currency and address other problems that had beset the economy ever since Agincourt. Such measures, as well as the reopening of trade with England, made Henry's regency synonymous with good government.

Despite the pockets of resistance, to many in France the treaty came as a welcome relief, representing as it did a resolution to years of civil unrest and division. It was especially welcome to the Burgundians, needless to say, who regarded it as a sure means of revenge against the Armagnacs. Henry rose to the challenge of ruling France, a testimony both to his ability to learn quickly and to immerse himself in French administration. Yet he could hardly overlook the fact that he was also King of England. The treaty marked a volte-face in English policies towards France. Hitherto Henry had encouraged a hostile stance, even xenophobia, especially in his dropping from the summer of 1417 onwards of Anglo-Norman in favour of English in his communications back home, which some have seen fit to call a 'language policy'.[12] Previously, he had emphasized Englishness and English supremacy, but that now sat uneasily with the terms of the treaty. While the English were happy supporting a war against the French, would they be quite so content with supporting the war which Henry was now waging as heir to the French throne against one faction in France? The treaty, moreover, reduced the prospect of land gains for soldiers and administrators now that the French were allies rather than conquered peoples, and required commanders and troops to collaborate with those who had previously been their enemies. For all that England had celebrated Henry's conquest of France, concerns about the new arrangements started to bubble up – and nowhere more so than in Parliament.

On 2 December 1420, at the opening of a new session of Parliament, the chancellor informed the assembled Lords and Commons that the king could not be present in person since he was 'busy overseas making good the situation there and working for the greater security of himself and his lieges of England'.[13] In another discussion, Parliament acknowledged that as heir and regent and, in time, King of France, Henry would inevitably 'sometimes be on this side of the sea and sometimes on the other, as seems best to him at his discretion'. A note of anxiety crept into debate on the matter, with the Commons putting forward five petitions relating to it. The first, indeed, stated simply that the king and queen should be encouraged to return to England soon 'for the comfort, relief and support of the Commons'. Despite the chancellor's assurances in his opening speech, the Commons were concerned that the king knew his personal presence in England was greatly desired, and – given the rival claim on his attention – wanted to know that Henry himself desired above everything else 'the prosperity and good governance of this kingdom'.[14]

But while Parliament had been encouraged to believe the king would soon be returning to England, given that 1 December was set for Henry's formal entry into Paris, and the Estates General and *lit de justice* were arranged for later in the month, such assurances were apparently disingenuous. Perhaps the Commons were annoyed at being misled. They petitioned successfully that should the king return during this or any future parliament, there would be no need for a dissolution or the calling of a new assembly: they were concerned that Henry would disrupt and undermine arrangements already made. Wider concerns are revealed in their request, also granted, that the statute of Edward III made in the parliament of 1340 following his adoption of the title King of France should be confirmed: this statute granted that the English should never be subjects of the King of England as King of France. While they spoke obsequiously of the king's acquisition of his new titles 'through the grace and powerful aid of God, and through his chivalrous, diligent and difficult labours',[15] their petition indicates that they did not think the Treaty of Troyes was explicit enough on guaranteeing English independence – and it was, undoubtedly, more concerned with the preservation of French liberties and identity.

There were two further issues on which the Commons expressed their concerns but were rebuffed. Early in the parliament, the keeper of the realm in the king's absence, Henry's brother Humphrey, Duke of Gloucester, told the Commons that petitions submitted to him would not be engrossed (ratified and enrolled) until they had been sent to the king overseas. In other words, Henry had not been prepared to delegate authority in his absence from the kingdom, something which for the Commons could only lead to delays in doing business. Replying to the Duke of Gloucester, they asked that all petitions should be 'answered and determined within the kingdom of England during the course of this same parliament', an arrangement that should apply to all future parliaments. Unsurprisingly, the answer came that the king's views should be sought.[16] The Commons, almost invariably protectionist by inclination, then put forward the ingenious argument that, now that Henry had both sides of the Channel in his hands, foreigners wishing to sail through should pay a toll. This was also rejected, as was their request for the upholding of a supposed ancient treaty that only English wool should be accepted for importation into Flanders. Measures like these could only lead to the alienation of the Duke of Burgundy, something the English crown could in no way afford now that he was a key ally.

Such were the Commons' anxieties over the Treaty of Troyes that no effort was made to have it ratified in Parliament, as its terms required, until the king was back in England. Similarly, it was deemed wise not to ask the Commons for a tax grant at this parliament. The chancellor admitted in his opening speech that bullion was in short supply because so much had gone overseas to pay for England's foreign wars. The years between 1415 and 1419 had been exceptionally heavily taxed, and Henry's desperate search for funds had led him to leave no stone unturned: it no doubt played a role in his treatment of his stepmother, Joan of Navarre, who was accused of witchcraft, thereby forfeiting her lands to the crown. In England, there were other signs of war weariness. Recruitment of men for expeditions was no longer as easy as it had been since the opportunities for profits were reduced. Efforts to raise troops in Norfolk in 1419 and Yorkshire and Lincolnshire in 1420 had elicited a variety of excuses as to why they did not want to serve: poverty, lack of horse and equipment, gout, dropsy. In Yorkshire only five out of ninety-six approached were willing: two men from Holderness said simply that they would do any service within the realm of England but would not go outside it.[17] Law and order was also emerging for the first time since 1414 as an issue, as revealed by a riot in Suffolk in July 1420.[18]

In theory, the king could rule England as an absentee. The machinery and practices of government were bureaucratic enough to allow this, but Henry tended to insist on matters being referred to him for approval. By the end of 1420, he had been absent from England continuously for over three years – something unparalleled in recent memory – which brought with it a real danger of a resentful country seeing itself as simply the milch cow for Henry's overseas ambitions. Reassurances had been given to the previous parliament in October 1419 that 'the king has a strong affection for his realm of England and wishes to know how the peace and the laws of the land and his officers there were managed in his absence; and if any of these things need amendment let this be provided by good and wise advice in this parliament'. But at the same time, immersed in initial discussions with the French following the murder at Montereau, Henry had the chancellor express to Parliament the point that if the war was discontinued because of lack of funds, the result would be disaster. Support had to be provided for the king 'so that he can feel that his people here look upon him and his estate at present with love and complete affection'.[19] The Commons on that occasion had been generous, granting a subsidy to be collected by 2 February 1420 and a third of a subsidy by the following 11 November. But we must wonder what the Commons at the parliament of December 1420 thought of the chancellor's opening speech which, while stressing Henry's achievements across his whole career and his concerns for the weakness and poverty of England, placed the onus on solving the problems completely on them: 'the wise Commons should invest all their labour so that through their actions . . . the means of providing effective solutions to the troubles and increasing the common benefit of the realm might be found'.[20]

It was becoming essential for Henry to return home, despite an equally pressing need for him to stay in France. A document detailing the careful preparations he made to cover his return to England shows his understanding of the issues as well as his attention to detail. He stipulated, for instance, that oaths to the Treaty of Troyes should be taken in Burgundian areas, including Flanders – indicating, perhaps, that he did not fully trust his allies. He was also interested in the security of the garrisons of Montereau and Melun, and the powers which the Dukes of Clarence and Exeter were to have in his absence. That the document, in French, was carefully scrutinized by Henry is indicated by the addition in his own hand of two notes in English: 'also to send to court for the abbot of Westminster', and 'also thither for the render of the Charterhouse'.[21] Such entries remind us again of his attempts to keep a close watch even on apparently small matters in England.

Henry and his queen finally landed at Dover on 1 February 1421. Following Catherine's coronation at Westminster, writs were sent out on 26 February for a parliament to meet on 2 May. That done, the king set out on progress. This was a significant decision on his part, revealing his awareness that not all his subjects saw the Troyes settlement as the outcome they had hoped for in the wars with France. While in England earlier in the reign, Henry had not itinerated as much as other kings, choosing to stay in the London area most of the time. Nor, save for the entry to London after Agincourt, had he sought opportunities for public spectacle. In late February 1421, Henry visited, initially alone, Bristol, Hereford and Shrewsbury, and then moved on to Kenilworth where Catherine joined him on 15 March.[22]

The Lancastrian Kenilworth Castle had been a special place for Henry ever since his childhood and became all the more special by virtue of his only royal building project, the creation of the Pleasance, a double-moated enclosure one hectare in extent, with living accommodation and gardens, on the edge of the Great Mere and half a mile to the north-west of the castle. Here 'in the marsh, where foxes hid among the prickly bushes and thorns, the king established a pleasure garden for his relaxation'.[23] This secret place could be accessed only by boat and could not be seen save from the tallest towers of the castle. It is highly significant that he should have Catherine meet him there. Based on the date of birth of their son, it was probably the place Henry VI was conceived. The king and queen moved on to Leicester together, then to Coventry, before coming back to Leicester for Easter. The couple then visited Nottingham and Pontefract, where the Duke of Orléans, Catherine's cousin and brother-in-law, was held.

Alone again, Henry then visited the shrines of St John of Beverley and St John of Bridlington. The former was connected with his victory at Agincourt – 25 October being his feast of translation – as it had been rumoured that oil had oozed from his tomb on the day of the battle, just as it had on the day Henry Bolingbroke had landed at Ravenspur in 1399. Passing by Newark, King's Lynn and Walsingham, Henry was back in Windsor by 28 April for the feast of the Order of the Garter.

As such progresses were designed to do, Henry's tour was an opportunity to show himself to his people and to emphasize his style of kingship: he heard petitions from the poor and distributed alms. But it was also a fundraising effort. On 8 April, when Henry was returning from Beverley to York, bad news came from France – his brother Thomas, Duke of Clarence had been defeated and killed in battle at Baugé in Anjou on 22 March – which not only made the king's early return to France more likely, but also prompted the appointment of commissioners to summon those who had not yet made loans to the crown. The Receipt Rolls show that £36,840 was raised, 'the highest combined loan of the century' and worth around the same as a full lay subsidy.[24] Over 530 lenders were involved, many from the areas through which Henry had passed, although half of the sum came from the immensely wealthy Henry Beaufort.

While such loans indicated continued public support for the war, Henry considered it wise not to ask the Commons in the parliament of May 1421 for a tax grant. With the king present, the Treaty of Troyes was ratified at a special meeting of the 'three estates of the realm' held during the parliament.[25] A bargain was struck with Parliament: in return for not being asked for money, the Commons would be prepared to vote a tax grant at the following parliament. The parliament also rubber-stamped Henry's annexation of the most valuable parts of the Bohun inheritance to which he had a claim through his mother, Mary de Bohun. Since she was co-heiress with her sister, Eleanor, who had married Thomas of Woodstock, the fifth son of Edward III, there needed to be a division of the lands, which Henry as king was able to exploit to his advantage.

While in England, Henry's thoughts never strayed far from France, and on progress he still played characteristically close attention even to the most specific of issues there. On 27 February, while at St Albans, he sent a letter responding to a query on whether masons and carpenters should be employed on the castle of Pontorson, in Lower Normandy, noting in the same letter that he had sent to the Earl of Suffolk instructions concerning the government of Avranches and its region.[26] Henry was equally wide-ranging in his scrutiny of matters in England. At Leicester he wrote to the monastic houses of the Benedictine Order in England ordering them to summon a meeting of monks at Westminster in early May, at which he appeared in person, berating the order for its laxity and urging reform.[27] Such a step reminds us that his regard for religion led him to intervene in Church matters, including the shaping of the monastic landscape, appointing bishops and repressing heresy, essentially acting, 'in all but name, as the supreme governor of the Church of England, more than a century before the title could be used'.[28]

On 10 June 1421, Henry landed at Calais with an army of 4,100 men, drawn largely from his personal estates in Cheshire and Lancashire. In the months that followed, he continued to fight and govern energetically. After a campaign that went as far south as Orléans, to assist the Duke of Burgundy's siege of Chartres, which had begun on 23 June but which the dauphin had abandoned on 5 July after hearing of the imminent arrival of the English king, Henry turned to the last remaining dauphinist stronghold near Paris, the well-fortified town of Meaux. The siege there proved longer than the one at Rouen, dragging on from 6 October 1421 to 10 May 1422. Henry was furious at the level of resistance put up first by the town and subsequently the area known as the Marché, and when it finally fell, was harsh in his treatment of its defenders, executing them rather than allowing the usual terms of ransom and honourable departure from the town. He also took 110 books from Meaux's religious establishments which he distributed to his monastic establishments in England.[29]

Catherine had become pregnant during the progress in the Midlands and did not return to France with her husband. On 6 December 1421, she gave birth to the desired male heir at Windsor, the news being celebrated in Paris with the ringing of bells and lighting of bonfires. As she travelled back to France in May 1422, she was welcomed at Mantes by streets strewn with sweet-smelling herbs.[30] The future did indeed seem rosy for the double monarchy. Catherine joined Henry in Paris on 29 May, but within a few weeks Henry's health was causing grave concern. From 7 July he was seriously ill, yet he continued to push himself: at Charenton he tried to reassure his followers that he was fit enough to play an active role by showing that he could still ride but the effort was too much. On 13 August, he arrived at the castle of Vincennes. He would never leave it.

The king was struggling with a serious intestinal condition – diagnosed by the French chronicler the Religieux of Saint-Denis as 'a disease of the flux of the belly'; for Monstrelet it was St Anthony's fire, or erysipelas, an acute infection which causes distinctive red inflammations of the skin and lymph nodes as well as fever and vomiting.[31] Henry continued to attempt to deal with business, fully aware that he was about to die. On 26 August, he made a codicil to the will he had drawn up just before he returned to France in June of the previous year, which superseded the one he had made before the Agincourt campaign. This new will gave the 'protection and defence' ('tutelam et defensionem') of his young heir, Prince Henry, to his brother Humphrey, Duke of Gloucester; however, it made the Duke of Exeter the prince's governor, also stipulating that his long-term and much trusted associates Henry, Lord Fitzhugh and Sir Walter Hungerford should be in the prince's household and about his person.[32] The vagueness of the powers accorded to the Duke of Gloucester was to cause problems during Henry VI's minority. Henry also laid down that the Duke of Orléans and the Count of Eu, two of the prisoners taken at Agincourt, should only be released with a large ransom and if they were willing to swear to accept the Treaty of Troyes.

As he lay close to death, chroniclers suggest, Henry gave further deathbed instructions to those gathered around him (who seem to have included the Duke of Exeter, the Earl of Warwick, his brother John and Louis Robessart), urging the continuation of the war until all of France accepted the Treaty of Troyes. There should be no treaty with the dauphin unless Normandy remained in English hands.[33] Finally, on 31 August, he died.

So shattering and unexpected was Henry's death, at the age of thirty-five, and such were the ramifications for England and English France – his heir was just shy of nine months old – that, according to one French writer, Perceval de Cagny, the English kept Henry's death secret for fifteen days, such was their fear of the effect it would have on loyalties.[34] Some claimed that Henry was cursed because he had moved religious relics from their rightful place; others that he had been inflicted by leprosy because of his policies. The Burgundian chronicler Georges Chastellain offered an alternative explanation for Henry's premature demise. According to him, a hermit had come in 1421 to ask Henry to stop afflicting the French, telling him that God had only allowed him to be so successful in his conquests because as prince he had been wounded in the forehead fighting heretics in England. But now it was God's will that if he did not stop he would die.[35]

Henry's body was eviscerated according to the usual practice, with his entrails being buried at Saint-Maur-des-Fossées. His corpse was taken to Calais via Saint-Denis and Rouen, where it was joined by Catherine, who would accompany it back to England. Its passage across northern France saw outpourings of grief as well as much ceremonial: at Rouen, the city he had starved into surrender, 200 townsmen all in black and each holding a torch, accompanied the horse-drawn hearse into the cathedral. Indeed, Henry's premature death was lamented in France since his wise and firm rule had offered a contrast with the anarchy caused by the divisions between Burgundians and Armagnacs and the mental incapacity of Charles VI. Reflecting on his demise, the Religieux of Saint-Denis called him 'magnanimous, valiant in arms, prudent, wise ... well regarded by the people'.[36] Mourning was equally great in England: the chronicler Thomas Walsingham spoke of Henry's subjects as being 'unspeakably distressed' that such a strong king and author of such remarkable deeds had been taken from them by God and that his successor was not yet a year old.[37]

Landing at Dover on 31 October 1422, the hearse was taken on the customary route through Canterbury to London, where it was received formally at Southwark on 5 November by the mayor, corporation and clergy, with 31 guilds paying for 211 torches. After procession to and display in St Paul's, it was escorted on 6 November to Westminster Abbey, with every house it passed displaying a torch in its honour. Henry was buried on 7 November in the location behind the high altar and close to the shrine of Edward the Confessor which he had specified as long ago as his first will of July 1415.[38] In his second will of June 1421, he had added a donation to the abbey of up to £4,000 for the completion of the 'new work' – the rebuilding of the nave. He had also added a donation of an altar cloth to the recluse of Westminster, asking him to pray especially for the king's soul.[39]

Although, in the few months between his death and his interment there had been some preparation of his tomb, the chantry chapel laid down in his will was not constructed until the 1430s. It displayed the king's religiosity – his constant emphasis on the Virgin, the Trinity, St George, St Edmund and St Edward the Confessor, supplemented by St Denis as a reflection of his French successes: the codicil to his will made five days before he died had added bequests of precious objects and a great cross which he had used on the altar in his own chapel.[40] The carvings placed on the sides of the chantry chapel also reflected the ways in which the king was recalled in the generation after his death. We see him portrayed in full motion on horseback in the field, before a fortress and crossing a river, representing his military successes. We also see two portrayals of his crowning, the double representation perhaps imagining the French crowning which he so nearly achieved. The scenes epitomize his own strong concepts of active and sacral kingship, and link back to his personal transformation at his accession. His wooden effigy on the tomb chest, portraying the king in parliament robes, lost its silver plating to robbery in the mid 1540s, and at some point its head and hands also disappeared. In the 1970s, these were both replaced by modern replicas, the head based on the well-known early Tudor portrait of Henry, the hands allegedly on those of Laurence Olivier.

A cynical view might be that Henry was assisted in terms of his reputation by his premature death. Had he lived he might have faced difficulties at home as much as in France, since it was by no means certain that the English would have been keen to pay for what had become, by the Treaty of Troyes, essentially a French civil war. His reign had seen eleven parliaments over nine years, the frequency reflecting his need for money: his reign was one of the most intensively taxed, paralleled only by the years 1377 to 1381 which triggered the Peasants' Revolt. But given his achievements to date, and his single-minded determination to succeed, who knows what might have happened? Had a double monarchy of England and France persisted, the future history of Europe would have been very different.

5
Epilogue

Henry V's life was short but packed full of activity, most of which was self-generated. He was one of England's busiest kings. His behaviour as prince was the product of impatience. He wanted to be king and was frustrated at his father's style of government. Having held the reins of power in 1410–11, he was doubly frustrated when they were taken from him, something which in turn triggered political misbehaviour as well as disengagement. After his accession he had much to disprove as well as prove. He took up the role of king with a vengeance, quickening the pace as well as the reach of royal government. He was resolved to get things done, whether it be in establishing law and order or in advancing the faith. He emphasized, but also drew strength from, his special relationship with God.

Henry grew in confidence over his years as king, learning from experience and gaining respect both at home and abroad for his firm but fair rule. He expected high standards from himself as well as from others. In France, he was conscious of the need to win hearts and minds as well as wars but did not shrink from using limited acts of cruelty to encourage submission. In England, too, he acted swiftly and harshly when challenged but also ensured the law was upheld and public order preserved for the benefit of the common good.

Such actions reveal a man of immense energy and foresight, as well as natural intelligence. Henry was able both to deal with many things at once and to give attention to detail. His surviving letters, through their lack of flowery language, demonstrate a brisk and direct style.[1] He was adroit in the use of written political communication, especially in his increasing use of English for public pronouncements, which persuaded at least one livery company, the Brewers, to adopt the vernacular in 1422 because the king had done so.[2]

Contemporaries saw him as a king of many talents. For the chronicler Thomas Walsingham he was, alongside his singular achievements as a warrior, monastic founder and devoted servant of God, 'sparing and discreet in word, astute in counsel, wise in judgement, modest in his looks but magnificent in action, steadfast in all he undertook to do'.[3] For John Strecche, at the Augustinian priory of Kenilworth, close to the special location which Henry created in the castle grounds for reflection and relaxation, Henry was

Julius in intellect, Hector in valour, Achilles in strength, Augustus in habits, with the eloquence of Paris ... another Solomon in judgement, a Troilus in the caring love of the heart ... if death had come to Henry V armed in the manner of a soldier, I believe Henry would have been the victor, for this king was never overcome in war.[4]

Notes

Unless drawn from an edition which includes an English translation, translations from works in French, Latin or Middle English are by the author of the current volume.

ABBREVIATIONS

Allmand	C. T. Allmand, *Henry V* (London: Eyre Methuen, 1992)
BL	British Library
CCR	*Calendar of Close Rolls*, 47 vols (London: 1900–1963)
CPR	*Calendar of Patent Rolls*, 53 vols (London: 1891–1916)
First English Life	*The First English Life of King Henry the Fifth*, ed. C. L. Kingsford (Oxford: Clarendon Press, 1911)
Gesta	*Gesta Henrici Quinti: The Deeds of Henry the Fifth*, ed. F. Taylor and J. S. Roskell (Oxford: Clarendon Press, 1975)
Mercer	M. Mercer, *Henry V: The Rebirth of Chivalry* (Kew: National Archives, 2004)
Monstrelet	*La Chronique d'Enguerran de Monstrelet*, ed. L. Douet-d'Arcq, 6 vols (Paris: Société de l'Histoire de France, 1857–62)
PPC	*Proceedings and Ordinances of the Privy Council of England 1368–1542*, ed. N. H. Nicolas, 7 vols (London: 1834–7)
PROME	*The Parliament Rolls of Medieval England 1275–1504*, ed. C. Given-Wilson (Woodbridge: 2005)
Pseudo-Elmham	*Thomae de Elmham Vita et Gesta Henrici Quinti*, ed. T. Hearne (Oxford: 1727)
Religieux	*La Chronique du religieux de Saint-Denis, contenant le règne de Charles VI de 1380 à 1422*, ed. L. Bellaguet, 6 vols (Paris: 1839–44)
Rymer	*Foedera, Conventiones, Litterae et Cuiuscunque Acta Publica*, ed. T. Rymer, 20 vols (London: 1704–35)
Tito Livio	*Titi Livii Foro-Juliensis Vita Henrici Quinti*, ed. T. Hearne (Oxford: 1716)
TNA	The National Archives, Kew
Walsingham	*The St Albans Chronicle*, II: *1394–1422*, ed. J. Taylor, W. Childs and L. Watkiss (Oxford: Clarendon Press, 2011)
Wylie	J. H. Wylie and W. T. Waugh, *The Reign of Henry V*, 3 vols (Cambridge: Cambridge University Press, 1914–29)

INTRODUCTION

1. *PROME*, IX, p. 249.
2. K. B. McFarlane, *Lancastrian Kings and Lollard Knights* (Oxford: Clarendon Press, 1972), p. 133.

1. FROM YOUNG LORD HENRY, TO PRINCE, TO POLITICAL OUTCAST

1. Allmand, pp. 7–8; TNA, DL 37/13, m. 6d, illustrated in Mercer, doc. 1. Henry was never called 'of Monmouth' until later centuries.
2. A. Weir, *Britain's Royal Families: The Complete Genealogy*, new edn (London: Pimlico, 2002), p. 124; I. Mortimer, *The Fears of Henry IV: England's Self-Made King* (London: Jonathan Cape, 2007), p. 371.
3. TNA, DL 28/1/1.
4. Allmand, pp. 9–10.
5. TNA, DL 28/1/4.
6. TNA, DL 28/1/6, fo. 39.
7. TNA, DL 28/3/5, fo. 14r.
8. TNA, DL 28/1/10, fo. 28r. Just before the date assigned for the duel, Henry and Thomas were sent from Kenilworth to Pontefract, where John of Gaunt was at the time, before returning to their father at Kenilworth.
9. TNA, E 403/561, m. 14, 16; E 403/562, m. 7 and 8.
10. TNA, E 404/16/394 (warrant of 5 March 1401); *Issues of the Exchequer*, ed. F. Devon (London: 1837), p. 218.
11. Walsingham, p. 151.
12. Pseudo-Elmham, p. 5.
13. The doubt comes from the fact that Richard may have dubbed him already during the Irish campaign and no one would be made a knight twice.
14. *PROME*, VIII, pp. 33–4.
15. 'Annales Ricardi Secondi et Henrici Quarti', in *Johannis de Trokelowe et Henrici de Blandeforde: Chronica et Annales*, ed. H. T. Riley, Rolls Series (London: 1866), p. 322.
16. All Souls College Oxford, MS 182, fo. 197b, printed in H. G. Richardson, 'Parliamentary Documents from Formularies', *Bulletin of the Institute of Historical Research*, 11 (1933–4), pp. 147–62.
17. *CPR, 1399–1401*, p. 392.
18. *Anglo-Norman Letters and Petitions*, ed. M. D. Legge, Anglo-Norman Text Society (Oxford: Blackwell, 1941), p. 301.
19. *CPR 1401–05*, p. 216.
20. *PPC*, II, pp. 62–3.
21. 'Annales Ricardi Secondi et Henrici Quarti', p. 361.
22. BL, Sloane MS 2272, fo. 137r.
23. *CCR, 1405–09*, p. 93.

24. *PROME*, VIII, pp. 330–31.
25. *PROME*, VIII, p. 341.
26. *PROME*, VIII, p. 347.
27. *PPC*, I, p. 295.
28. *PROME*, VIII, pp. 366–75.
29. D. Pearsall, 'Hoccleve's *Regement of Princes*: The Poetics of Royal Self-Representation', *Speculum*, 69 (1994), pp. 386–410, and L. Mooney, 'A Holograph Copy of Thomas Hoccleve's *Regiment of Princes*', *Studies in the Age of Chaucer*, 33 (2011), pp. 263–96. I am grateful to Dr Jenni Nuttall for discussion on this text and others of Henry's books.
30. Cambridge, Trinity College, MS B 15.23, fo. 16v–22r.
31. *PPC*, II, pp. 19–24, 33–4.
32. TNA, SC 6/775/12 m. 2d.
33. *Incerti Scriptoris Chronicon Angliae de Regnis Trium Regum Lancastriensium*, ed. J. A. Giles (London: 1848), p. 63.
34. 'Continuatio Eulogii', in *Eulogium Historiarum Sive Temporis*, ed. F. S. Haydon, Rolls Series (London: 1863), III, pp. 420–21, although misdating this to 1413.
35. *PROME*, VIII, p. 519.
36. Walsingham, pp. 611–15.
37. Ibid.
38. *First English Life*, p. 13. I am grateful to Professor Maria Hayward for discussion on the prince's robe.
39. Walsingham, p. 615.
40. Tito Livio, p. 5; Pseudo-Elmham, pp. 13–15; *First English Life*, pp. 13–16.
41. For instance, *Jean de Waurin: Receuil des croniques et anciennes istories de la Grant Bretagne, 1399–1422*, ed. W. Hardy, Rolls Series (London: 1868), pp. 159–60.
42. *Political Poems and Songs Relating to English History*, ed. T. Wright, Rolls Series (London: 1861), II, pp. 120–21.
43. Pseudo-Elmham, p. 14.
44. New York, Pierpont Morgan Library, MS M.81, which bears the prince's arms as he held them after 1406 when Henry IV adopted the French form of fleur-de-lys.
45. Twenty-seven manuscripts survive, including BL Cotton Vespasian B.xii, which formed the basis of the 1904 printed edition of the work. To date, it has not been possible to link any particular manuscript to the ownership of Prince Henry.
46. Tito Livio, p. 4; Pseudo-Elmham, p. 12. It may be that the screen at York Minster portrays the king towards the end of his life.
47. TNA, SC 6/813/23.
48. TNA, E 101/406/21, fo. 23 (Sir John Oldcastle, August 1413); *Records of the City of Norwich*, ed. W. Hudson and J. C. Tingay (London: Jarrold and Sons, 1910), II, p. 61 (Sir Thomas Erpingham, 1413–14).

2. NEW KING, NEW MAN

1. Walsingham, pp. 619–21.
2. Titi Livio, p. 5; Pseudo-Elmham, p. 14.
3. TNA, E 404/30/117, cited in Allmand, p. 350.
4. TNA, E 101/406/21, fo. 19.

5. D. Knowles, *The Religious Orders in England*, II: *The End of the Middle Ages* (Cambridge: Cambridge University Press, 1955), p. 367. Regarded as a particularly holy hermit, Alnwick later became confessor-general in the Bridgettine house which Henry founded.

6. Rymer, IX, p. 289.

7. Pseudo-Elmham, p. 15.

8. *First English Life*, p. 5; L. Mirot, 'Le procès de maître Jean Fusoris', *Mémoires de la société de l'histoire de Paris et de l'Ile de France*, 27 (1900), p. 244.

9. Mirot, 'Le procès de maître Jean Fusoris', p. 175.

10. Rymer, X, p. 317. It subsequently went to Henry's Charterhouse at Sheen.

11. S. McKendrick, J. Lowden and K. Doyle, *Royal Manuscripts: The Genius of Illumination* (London: British Library, 2011), pp. 156–7. The copy at Cambridge Corpus Christi College, MS 213, may be that written for the king, with BL Royal MS 20.B.iv intended for him to present as a gift.

12. TNA, E 101/335/17, listed in K. B. McFarlane, *Lancastrian Kings and Lollard Knights*, pp. 233–8; P. and F. Strong, 'The Last Will and Codicils of Henry V', *English Historical Review*, 96 (1981), pp. 93–100.

13. Headed 'le roy Henry', BL, Additional MS 57,950, fo. 12v. The Gloria was recorded by the Binchois Consort: 'Music for Henry V and the House of Lancaster', Hyperion CDA67868 2011. Henry IV has also been proposed as the composer.

14. *The Brut, or The Chronicles of England*, ed. F. W. D. Brie, Early English Text Society, Original Series 131 and 136 (London: 1906–8), II, p. 594.

15. G. Dodd, 'Henry V's Establishment: Service, Loyalty and Reward in 1413', in *Henry V: New Interpretations*, ed. G. Dodd (Woodbridge: Boydell Press, 2013), p. 44.

16. *PROME*, VIII, p. 40.

17. Dodd, 'Henry V's Establishment', p. 39.

18. TNA, E 403/612 (payment enrolled at the Exchequer on 4 May).

19. TNA, E 101/406/21; Wylie, I, pp. 208–10.

20. TNA, E 403/612 (payments enrolled on 31 May and 4 July).

21. J. Stratford, 'The Royal Library in England Before the Reign of Edward IV', in *England in the Fifteenth Century: Proceedings of the 1992 Harlaxton Symposium*, ed. N. Rogers (Stamford: Paul Watkins, 1994), p. 194. The bible is BL, Royal MS 1.E.ix (*c.*1410–15); Strong, 'Last Will', p. 93.

22. TNA, E 403/612 (under 20 May).

23. *CPR, 1413–16*, p. 45; *CCR, 1413–19*, p. 20.

24. *PROME*, IX, p. 9; VIII, p. 461. Henry kept to his word. Over the course of his reign the annuity bill was 'reduced to £12,000 p.a., half the figure under Henry IV': G. L. Harris, 'Financial Policy', in *Henry V: The Practice of Kingship*, ed. G. L. Harris (Oxford: Oxford University Press, 1985), p. 174.

25. C. Given-Wilson, 'Introduction to the Parliament of 1413', *PROME*, IX, p. 3.

26. *PROME*, IX, p. 7.

27. *PROME*, IX, p. 8.

28. *PROME*, IX, pp. 36–7.

29. *PROME*, IX, p. 37.

30. TNA, E 101/406/21 fo. 23.

31. Ibid.

32. Allmand, p. 299.

33. *The History of Parliament: The House of Commons, 1386–1421*, ed. J. S. Roskell, L. Clark and C. Rawcliffe (Stroud: Alan Sutton for the History of Parliament Trust, 1992), II, p. 534.

34. Walsingham, p. 663.
35. Walsingham, p. 729.
36. Allmand, p. 273.
37. Cited in Allmand, pp. 275–6. Plans in August 1414 for a third monastic foundation, a Celestine house modelled on that at Paris, were impossible to implement once war with France started.
38. Religieux, V, p. 161.
39. Religieux, V, pp. 158–61.
40. Walsingham, p. 645.
41. Lille, Archives du Nord, B 423, no. 15319, printed in J. H. Wylie, 'Memorandum Concerning a Proposed Marriage between Henry V and Catherine of France in 1414', *English Historical Review*, 29 (1914), pp. 323–4.
42. Rymer, IX, pp. 131–2.
43. *PROME*, IX, p. 66.
44. 'Liber Metricus de Henrico Quinto, by Thomas Elmham', in *Memorials of Henry the Fifth, King of England*, ed. C. A. Cole, Rolls Series (London: 1858), p. 101.
45. Wylie, I, p. 315.
46. G. Hilton, *The Deeds of Henry V, as Told by John Strecche* (Kenilworth: privately printed, 2014), pp. 5–6; F. Taylor, 'The Chronicle of John Strecche for the Reign of Henry V (1414–1422)', *Bulletin of the John Rylands Library*, 16 (1932), p. 150.
47. L. Mirot, 'Autour de la paix d'Arras (1414–1415)', *Annales de Bourgogne*, 3 (1931), p. 320.
48. Mirot, 'Le procès de maître Jean Fusoris', pp. 175, 236.
49. *Gesta*, p. 17. One of these copies survives in TNA, E 30/1695, dated at Titchfield Abbey on 10 July 1415.
50. *PPC*, II, p. 151.
51. J. Stratford, '*Par le special commandement du roy*: Jewels and Plate Pledged for the Agincourt Expedition', in Dodd (ed.), *Henry V: New Interpretations*, pp. 157–70.
52. *PPC*, II, p. 148.
53. *PPC*, II, pp. 125, 157.
54. Mirot, 'Le procès de maître Jean Fusoris', pp. 247–9.
55. T. B. Pugh, *Henry V and the Southampton Plot of 1415*, Southampton Records Series 30 (Southampton: Southampton University Press, 1988), p. 163.

3. AGINCOURT AND NORMANDY

1. *PROME*, IX, p. 67.
2. *Gesta*, pp. 34–5.
3. *Gesta*, p. 25.
4. Rymer, IX, p. 317.
5. *Gesta*, p. 61.
6. *Gesta*, p. 75.
7. *Gesta*, p. 79.
8. A. Curry, *The Battle of Agincourt: Sources and Interpretations*, 2nd edn (Woodbridge: Boydell Press, 2009), p. 475.
9. *PROME*, IX, p. 115.

10. *Gesta*, p. 103.

11. *Gesta*, p. 107.

12. *Gesta*, p. 111.

13. Curry, *Sources*, pp. 271–4.

14. *PPC*, II, pp. 196–7.

15. TNA, E 403/622 m. 9.

16. Tito Livio, p. 25; Pseudo-Elmham, pp. 78–9.

17. TNA, E 30/1609, 1068, 1273; *Monstrelet*, III, p. 63

18. *PROME*, IX, p. 178.

19. Curry, *Sources*, pp. 448–9.

20. *PROME*, IX, p. 185.

21. *PROME*, IX, pp. 196–7.

22. *The Register of Henry Chichele, Archbishop of Canterbury, 1414–1443*, ed. E. F. Jacob (London: Canterbury and York Society, 1938–47), III, pp. 28–9.

23. *PROME*, IX, p. 207.

24. *Calendar of the Letter Books of the City of London*, ed. R. R. Sharpe, *Letter Book I* (London: Corporation of London, 1909), pp. 71–2.

25. *PPC*, II, p. 353.

26. *Chronique de Jean Le Fèvre, Seigneur de Saint-Rémy*, ed. F. Morand (Paris: Société de l'Histoire de France, 1876), I, p. 348.

27. Rymer, IX, p. 752.

28. Rymer, IX, p. 779.

29. M. G. A. Vale, *Charles VII* (London: Eyre Methuen, 1974), p. 28.

30. Cited in Vale, *Charles VII*, p. 14.

4. HEIR AND REGENT OF FRANCE

1. Quotations from the treaty are taken from the English translation by A. Curry, 'Two Kingdoms, One King: The Treaty of Troyes (1420) and the Creation of a Double Monarchy of England and France', in *The Contesting Kingdoms: France and England 1420–1700*, ed. G. Richardson (Aldershot: Ashgate Press, 2008), pp. 23–41.

2. P. Bonenfant, *Du meurtre de Montereau au traité de Troyes* (Brussels: Académie Royale de Belgique, 1958), p. 192.

3. Bonenfant, *Du meurtre de Montereau*, p. 193.

4. TNA, C 54/270 m. 17d, with a facsimile in Mercer, doc. 13.

5. Curry, 'Two Kingdoms', p. 38.

6. TNA C 47/30/9/10, with a facsimile in Mercer, doc. 14.

7. *Monstrelet*, III, p. 403.

8. The account of the entry to Paris is in *Journal d'un bourgeois de Paris 1405–1449*, ed. A. Tuetey (Paris: Champion, 1881), p. 163.

9. *The Great Chronicle of London*, ed. A. H. Thomas and I. D. Thornley (London: George W. Jones, 1938), p. 118.

10. A. Longnon, *Paris pendant la domination anglaise (1420–1436)* (Paris: Champion, 1878), p. 32.

11. Rymer, X, pp. 30–32.

12. J. Fisher, 'A Language Policy for Lancastrian England', *Proceedings of the Modern Language Association of America*, 107 (1992), pp. 1168–80; M. Richardson, 'Henry V, the English Chancery and Chancery English', *Speculum*, 55 (1980), pp. 726–50.

13. *PROME*, IX, p. 249.

14. *PROME*, IX, p. 251.

15. *PROME*, IX, pp. 258–9.

16. *PROME*, IX, p. 260.

17. *PPC*, II, p. 247; A. E. Goodman, 'Responses in Yorkshire for Military Service under Henry V', *Northern History*, 17 (1981), pp. 240–52. For similar problems in Lincolnshire, see TNA, E 101/55/13.

18. *PPC*, II, p. 272.

19. *PROME*, IX, p. 231.

20. *PROME*, IX, p. 249.

21. TNA, E 30/1619, with a facsimile in Mercer, doc. 15.

22. TNA, C 81/667/993; *CPR, 1416–22*, p. 318. For a map of the progress, see J. Doig, 'Propaganda and Truth: Henry V's Royal Progress in 1421', *Nottingham Medieval Studies*, 40 (1996), p. 173.

23. 'Liber Metricus de Henrico Quinto', pp. 100–101; E. Jamieson and R. Lane, 'The Pleasance, Kenilworth: A Royal Residence and Pleasure Garden', *English Heritage Research News*, 19 (2013), pp. 26–9.

24. TNA, E 401/696.

25. *PROME*, IX, p. 278.

26. Bibliothèque Nationale de France, nouvelles acquisitions françaises, 344, no. 21, printed in R. A. Newhall, *The English Conquest of Normandy 1416–1424: A Study in Fifteenth Century Warfare* (New Haven: Russell and Russell, 1924), p. 266.

27. W. A. Pantin, *Documents Illustrating the Activities of the General and Provincial Chapters of the English Black Monks 1215–1540*, Camden 3rd Series (London: 1933), II, pp. 104–5.

28. J. Catto, 'Religious Change under Henry V', in *Henry V: The Practice of Kingship*, ed. Harris, p. 115.

29. J. Stratford, 'The Royal Library in England Before the Reign of Edward IV', in *England in the Fifteenth Century: Proceedings of the 1992 Harlaxton Symposium*, ed. N. Rogers (Stamford: Paul Watkins, 1994), p. 193.

30. J. Shirley, *A Parisian Journal 1405–1449* (Oxford: Clarendon Press, 1968), p. 166; Archives Communales de Mantes, CC 20, fo. 25.

31. *Religieux*, VI, p. 480; *Monstrelet*, IV, p. 109.

32. *Strong*, 'Last Will', pp. 99–100.

33. *Monstrelet*, IV, p. 110.

34. *Chroniques de Perceval de Cagny*, ed. H. Moranvillé (Paris: Société de l'Histoire de France, 1902), p. 126.

35. Wylie, III, pp. 418–19.

36. *Religieux*, VI, p. 480.

37. *Walsingham*, p. 775.

38. Rymer, IX, p. 289; Strong, 'Last Will', pp. 89–90.

39. Strong, 'Last Will', pp. 92, 93.

40. Strong, 'Last Will', p. 100.

5. EPILOGUE

1. For instance, BL Cotton MS Vespasian F.iii, fo. 8, written from France in 1418 or 1419.
2. *The Book of London English 1384–1435*, ed. E. Chambers and M. Daunt (Oxford: Clarendon Press, 1967), p. 16. Ironically, the decision is recorded in Latin.
3. Walsingham, p. 773.
4. Taylor, 'Chronicle of John Strecche', p. 187.

Further Reading

The best and fullest biography of Henry is C. T. Allmand, *Henry V* (London: Eyre Methuen, 1992), which now forms part of the Yale English Monarchs series. In 1968 Professor Allmand published a useful pamphlet on Henry V for the Historical Association (General Series, no. 68). Reissued in a revised edition in 2013, it provides a succinct historiographical guide to works on the king. For general context, nothing beats G. L. Harris, *Shaping the Nation: England 1360–1461* (Oxford: Oxford University Press, 2005), in the New Oxford History of England series.

J. H. Wylie's three-volume *The Reign of Henry V* (Cambridge: Cambridge University Press, 1914–29) is still much quoted and includes fascinating detail but fails to discriminate between the sources on which it draws. Wylie died before it could be completed; the third volume was written by W. T. Waugh based on his notes. The whole work is now available freely online at the Internet Archive (archive.org). C. L. Kingsford produced a biography, *Henry V: The Typical Medieval Hero* (London and New York: Putnam, 1901; 2nd edn 1923). Given the author's expertise in the chronicle sources, this remains a valuable work. Kingsford also edited an important work of 1513–14, *The First English Life of Henry V* (Oxford: Clarendon Press, 1911).

There are a number of more popular biographies which provide lively if sometimes uncritical accounts of the king. Among these are H. F. Hutchinson, *Henry V* (London: Eyre and Spottiswoode, 1967), P. Earle, *The Life and Times of Henry V* (London: Weidenfeld & Nicolson, 1972), and D. Seward, *Henry V as Warlord* (Harmondsworth: Penguin, 1987). More substantial is K. Dockray, *Warrior King:*

The Life of Henry V (Stroud: History Press, 2006), and J. Matusiak, *Henry V* (London: Routledge, 2013), along with the short, as appropriate for the Pocket Giants series, A. J. Pollard, *Henry V* (Stroud: History Press, 2014). An attractive format is provided by M. Mercer, *Henry V: The Rebirth of Chivalry* (Kew: National Archives, 2004), which, as its series title suggests (English Monarchs: Treasures from the National Archives), prints and discusses facsimiles of documents from the royal records.

There are stimulating chapters on the relationship between Henry and his father, as well as a personal view of Henry V in K. B. McFarlane's *Lancastrian Kings and Lollard Knights* (Oxford: Clarendon Press, 1972). Equally valuable is T. B. Pugh, *Henry V and the Southampton Plot of 1415*, first published as volume 30 in the Southampton Records Series (Southampton: Southampton University Press, 1988). In addition to discussion of the plot and appendices with the confessions of those involved, Dr Pugh provides a critical view of the king. *Henry V: The Practice of Kingship*, edited by G. L. Harris (Oxford: Oxford University Press, 1985), also contains an overview as well as chapters on various aspects of the reign written by specialists. A second collection of essays, *Henry V: New Interpretations*, edited by G. Dodd (Woodbridge: Boydell Press, 2013), provides insights into where historians are now going in studies of Henry V. Fuller consideration of Henry's religious and intellectual leanings, and notions of kingship, is to be found in M. G. A. Vale, *Henry V: The Conscience of a King* (Newhaven and London: Yale University Press, 2016).

For Henry as prince, a good starting point is J. H. Wylie's four-volume *History of England under Henry the Fourth* (London: Longmans, Green, 1884–98), as well as P. McNiven, *Heresy and Politics in the Reign of Henry IV: The Burning of John Badby* (Woodbridge: Boydell Press, 1987), to which should be added Dr McNiven's seminal articles 'Prince Henry and the English Political Crisis of 1412', *History*, 65 (1980), and 'The Problem of Henry IV's Health, 1405–1413', *English Historical Review*, 100 (1985). My chapter 'The Making of a Prince:

The Finances of the "Young Lord Henry", 1386–1400', in Dodd's *Henry V: New Interpretations*, gives more material on some of the points made in the current volume. For Henry in Wales, R. R. Davies, *The Revolt of Owain Glyndŵr* (Oxford and New York: Oxford University Press, 1995), is essential, with further detail in articles by R. Griffiths: 'Prince Henry's War: Armies, Garrisons and Supply During the Glyndŵr Rising', *Bulletin of the Board of Celtic Studies*, 34 (1987), and 'Prince Henry and Wales', in *Profit, Piety and Professions in Late Medieval England*, edited by M. Hicks (Gloucester: Alan Sutton, 1991).

Agincourt has stimulated by far the largest concentration of works on any topic of Henry's reign. Serious interest began with N. H. Nicolas, *History of the Battle of Agincourt* (London: 1827; 2nd edn 1832; 3rd edn 1833). In 2000, I published *The Battle of Agincourt: Sources and Interpretations* (Woodbridge: Boydell Press; 2nd edn 2009; e-book 2015), and in 2005 a full scholarly study of the battle, *Agincourt: A New History* (Stroud: Tempus Publishing, now published by the History Press). Also in 2005 appeared J. Barker's lively and more populist *Agincourt: The King, the Campaign, the Battle* (London: Little, Brown, 2005). I. Mortimer's *1415: Henry V's Year of Glory* (London: Bodley Head, 2009) sets the battle in the context of the year as a whole, using an ingenious day-by-day approach which brings out the complexity of royal life and action. C. J. Rogers has contributed two important articles to the Agincourt debate: 'Henry V's Military Strategy in 1415', in *The Hundred Years War: A Wider Focus*, edited by L. J. A. Villalon and D. J. Kagay (Leiden: Brill, 2005), and 'The Battle of Agincourt', in the second volume of this work (published in 2008). The third volume (published in 2013) contains my chapter 'Harfleur under English Rule 1415–1422', while a study of the town's rescue can be found in my 'After Agincourt, What Next? Henry V and the Campaign of 1416', *Fifteenth Century England*, 7 (2007). Henry's triumphal entry into London is reconstructed in N. Coldstream, 'Pavilion'd in Splendour: Henry V's Agincourt Pageants', *Journal of the British Archaeological Association*, 165 (2012).

For Henry V's soldiers, many are listed on www.medievalsoldier.org and discussed in A. Bell, A. Curry, A. King and D. Simpkin, *The Soldier in Later Medieval England* (Oxford: Clarendon Press, 2013). Henry's interest in military matters is discussed in my 'The Military Ordinances of Henry V: Texts and Contexts', in *War, Government and Aristocracy in the British Isles c.1150–1500*, edited by C. Given-Wilson, A. Kettle and L. Scales (Woodbridge: Boydell Press, 2008), and in C. Taylor, 'Henry V, Flower of Chivalry', in Dodd's *Henry V: New Interpretations*. On the king's treatment of the Harfleur and Agincourt prisoners, there are three important contributions by R. Ambühl: 'A Fair Share of the Profits? The Ransoms of Agincourt', *Nottingham Medieval Studies*, 50 (2006); 'Le sort des prisonniers d'Azincourt', *Revue du Nord*, 89 (2007); and *Prisoners of War in the Hundred Years War: Ransom Culture in the Late Middle Ages* (Cambridge: Cambridge University Press, 2013).

For a wide-ranging collection of essays, which includes discussion of military matters, my *Agincourt 1415: Henry V, Sir Thomas Erpingham and the Triumph of the English Archers* (Stroud: Tempus Publishing 2000), reissued as *Agincourt 1415: The Archer's Story* (Stroud: History Press, 2008), is valuable and well illustrated, as is M. Strickland and R. Hardy, *The Great Warbow* (Stroud: Alan Sutton, 2005), with stimulating chapters on the battle and its archers. This can be supplemented by the catalogue for the 2015 exhibition at the Tower of London, *The Battle of Agincourt*, edited by A. Curry and M. Mercer (London: Yale University Press, 2015).

Henry's later campaigns and the Treaty of Troyes are included in J. Barker, *Conquest: The English Kingdom of France 1417–1450* (London: Little, Brown, 2009). A scholarly account is provided by R. A. Newhall, *The English Conquest of Normandy 1416–1424: A Study in Fifteenth Century Warfare* (New Haven, Conn.: Yale University Press, 1924), C. T. Allmand, *Lancastrian Normandy: The History of a Medieval Occupation* (Oxford: Clarendon Press, 1983), and G. L. Thompson, *Paris and Its People under English Rule: The*

Anglo-Burgundian Regime 1420–1436 (Oxford: Clarendon Press, 1991), supplemented by my article 'Lancastrian Normandy: The Jewel in the Crown?', in *England and Normandy in the Middle Ages*, edited by D. Bates and A. Curry (London: Hambledon Press, 1994). Although Henry never went to the English lands in south-west France, they were an important part of national interest: a full discussion is provided in M. G. A. Vale, *English Gascony 1399–1453: A Study of War, Government and Politics During the Later Stages of the Hundred Years War* (Oxford: Clarendon Press, 1970), with the Gascon rolls online at www.gasconrolls.org.

For the highly complex French politics of the period, try R. Famiglietti, *Royal Intrigue: Crisis at the Court of Charles VI, 1392–1420* (New York: AMS Press, 1986), as well as J. Sumption, *Cursed Kings: The Hundred Years War IV* (London: Faber & Faber, 2015), which also contains a good account of Henry's campaigns. The importance of the dukes of Burgundy to Henry's interests and policies in France are well covered in biographies of the two dukes with whom he interacted: R. Vaughn, *John the Fearless: The Growth of Burgundian Power* (London: Longmans, 1966); and R. Vaughn, *Philip the Good: The Apogee of Burgundy* (London: Longmans, 1970). Both are now published by the Boydell Press.

Biographies of other key individuals can also provide interesting routes into the reign. C. Given-Wilson, *Henry IV* (Newhaven and London: Yale University Press, 2016), provides an excellent insight into Henry's father. Two of Henry's brothers (John and Humphrey) have biographies, although rather dated: E. Carleton-Williams, *My Lord of Bedford 1389–1453* (London: Longmans, 1963); and K. H. Vickers, *Humphrey, Duke of Gloucester* (London: Constable, 1907). His clergy have been better served: E. F. Jacob, *Henry Chichele and the Ecclesiastical Politics of his Age* (London: Athlone Press, 1952); M. Aston, *Thomas Arundel: A Study of Church Life in the Reign of Richard II* (Oxford: Clarendon Press, 1967); and especially G. L. Harris, *Cardinal Beaufort: A Study of Lancastrian Ascendancy and Decline* (Oxford: Clarendon Press, 1988). For other key individuals, the *Oxford Dictionary of National Biography* is essential, with further detailed biographies of MPs in *History of Parliament: The Commons 1386–1422*, edited by J. S. Roskell, L. S. Clark and C. Rawcliffe, 4 vols (Gloucester: Alan Sutton for the History of Parliament Trust, 1992).

On Henry's government there are several useful articles in Dodd's collection of essays *Henry V: New Interpretations*, including G. Dodd, 'Henry V's Establishment: Service, Loyalty and Reward in 1413', and W. M. Ormrod, 'Henry V and the English Taxpayer'. On finance, the best general summary is in A. Steel, *The Receipt of the Exchequer 1377–1485* (Cambridge: Cambridge University Press, 1954), with J. Stratford, '*Par le special commandement du roy*: Jewels and Plate Pledged for the Agincourt Expedition', in the Dodd collection as a fascinating glimpse into the special arrangements in 1415. E. Powell, *Kingship, Law and Society: Criminal Justice in the Reign of Henry V* (Oxford: Clarendon Press, 1989), provides a full study of the king's attempts to improve law and order. *The Parliament Rolls of Medieval England 1275–1504*, IX: *Henry V*, edited by C. Given-Wilson (Woodbridge: Boydell Press, 2005), includes contextual introductions as well as parallel texts.

The best overview of Henry's monastic foundations remains D. Knowles, *The Religious Orders in England*, II: *The End of the Middle Ages* (Cambridge: Cambridge University Press, 1955), with valuable studies of the Lollards by A. Hudson, *The Premature Reformation* (Oxford: Clarendon Press, 1988), and J. A. F. Thomson, *The Later Lollards 1414–1520* (Oxford: Clarendon Press, 1965), expanded by M. Jurkowski's chapter in the Dodd collection: 'Henry V's Suppression of the Oldcastle Revolt'. For general background, G. Bernard, *The Late Medieval English Church: Vitality and Vulnerability before the Break with Rome* (London: Yale University Press, 2013), is useful. Much can also be elucidated on Henry's religion by considering his preparations for death through reading P. and F. Strong, 'The Last Will and Codicils of Henry V', *English Historical Review*, 96 (1981), and W. St John Hope, 'The Funeral, Monument and Chantry Chapel of King Henry the Fifth', *Archaeologia*, 63 (1913–14).

Henry is not well served in terms of cultural history but insights can be gained through J. E. Krochalis, 'The Books and Reading of Henry V and His Circle', *Chaucer Review*, 23 (1988), and, for manuscripts, S. McKendrick, J. Lowden and K. Doyle, *Royal Manuscripts: The Genius of Illumination* (London: British Library, 2011). For his buildings, see *The History of the King's Works*, I and II: *The Middle Ages*, edited by H. Colvin (London: HMSO, 1963). On his image as projected in the chronicles of the period, A. Gransden, *Historical Writing in England*, II: *c.1307 to the Early Sixteenth Century* (London: Routledge, 1982), is the essential guide.

Picture Credits

1. Fifteenth-century manuscript of Edward, Duke of York's *Master of the Game*. BL Cotton Vespasian B.xii (© The British Library Board)

2. 'Gloria', composed by King ('Roy') Henry. Old Hall manuscript, BL Add MS 57, 950 f. 12v (© British Library Board. All Rights Reserved/Bridgeman Images)

3. John Bradmore's sketch showing the surgical instrument he made to remove a barbed arrowhead from Prince Henry's right cheek. BL Sloane 2272 folio 137r (© The British Library Board)

4. Thomas Hoccleve's *The Regiment of Princes*. BL Royal D vi f. 40 (© The British Library Board)

5. Imagined depiction of the Battle of Agincourt. Fifteenth-century book illumination from *Abrégé de la Chronique d'Enguerran de Monstrelet*. Ms. français 2680, fol. 208r (akg-images/Jérôme da Cunha)

6. The Great Bible, mentioned in Henry V's will. BL Royal 1 E ix (© The British Library Board)

7. Autograph letter of Henry V. BL Cotton Vespasian F.iii f. 8 (© The British Library Board)

8. The castle of Vincennes, east of Paris, scene of Henry V's death (© Bruno De Hogues/Getty Images)

9. Tudor portrait of Henry V, unknown artist (© National Portrait Gallery, London)

Index

Penguin Monarchs

THE HOUSES OF WESSEX AND DENMARK

THE HOUSES OF NORMANDY, BLOIS AND ANJOU

THE HOUSE OF PLANTAGENET

THE HOUSES OF LANCASTER AND YORK

* Now in paperback

THE HOUSE OF TUDOR

Henry VII	Sean Cunningham
Henry VIII*	John Guy
Edward VI*	Stephen Alford
Mary I*	John Edwards
Elizabeth I	Helen Castor

THE HOUSE OF STUART

James I	Thomas Cogswell
Charles I*	Mark Kishlansky
[Cromwell*	David Horspool]
Charles II*	Clare Jackson
James II	David Womersley
William III & Mary II*	Jonathan Keates
Anne	Richard Hewlings

THE HOUSE OF HANOVER

George I	Tim Blanning
George II	Norman Davies
George III	Amanda Foreman
George IV	Stella Tillyard
William IV	Roger Knight
Victoria*	Jane Ridley

THE HOUSES OF SAXE-COBURG & GOTHA AND WINDSOR

Edward VII*	Richard Davenport-Hines
George V*	David Cannadine
Edward VIII*	Piers Brendon
George VI*	Philip Ziegler
Elizabeth II*	Douglas Hurd

* Now in paperback

ALLEN LANE
an imprint of
PENGUIN BOOKS

Also Published

Stephen Kotkin, *Stalin, Vol. II: Waiting for Hitler, 1928-1941*

Lindsey Fitzharris, *The Butchering Art: Joseph Lister's Quest to Transform the Grisly World of Victorian Medicine*

Serhii Plokhy, *Lost Kingdom: A History of Russian Nationalism from Ivan the Great to Vladimir Putin*

Mark Mazower, *What You Did Not Tell: A Russian Past and the Journey Home*

Lawrence Freedman, *The Future of War: A History*

Niall Ferguson, *The Square and the Tower: Networks, Hierarchies and the Struggle for Global Power*

Matthew Walker, *Why We Sleep: The New Science of Sleep and Dreams*

Edward O. Wilson, *The Origins of Creativity*

John Bradshaw, *The Animals Among Us: The New Science of Anthropology*

David Cannadine, *Victorious Century: The United Kingdom, 1800-1906*

Leonard Susskind and Art Friedman, *Special Relativity and Classical Field Theory*

Maria Alyokhina, *Riot Days*

Oona A. Hathaway and Scott J. Shapiro, *The Internationalists: And Their Plan to Outlaw War*

Chris Renwick, *Bread for All: The Origins of the Welfare State*

Anne Applebaum, *Red Famine: Stalin's War on Ukraine*

Richard McGregor, *Asia's Reckoning: The Struggle for Global Dominance*

Chris Kraus, *After Kathy Acker: A Biography*

Clair Wills, *Lovers and Strangers: An Immigrant History of Post-War Britain*

Odd Arne Westad, *The Cold War: A World History*

Max Tegmark, *Life 3.0: Being Human in the Age of Artificial Intelligence*

Jonathan Losos, *Improbable Destinies: How Predictable is Evolution?*

Chris D. Thomas, *Inheritors of the Earth: How Nature Is Thriving in an Age of Extinction*

Chris Patten, *First Confession: A Sort of Memoir*

James Delbourgo, *Collecting the World: The Life and Curiosity of Hans Sloane*

Naomi Klein, *No Is Not Enough: Defeating the New Shock Politics*

Ulrich Raulff, *Farewell to the Horse: The Final Century of Our Relationship*

Slavoj Žižek, *The Courage of Hopelessness: Chronicles of a Year of Acting Dangerously*

Patricia Lockwood, *Priestdaddy: A Memoir*

Ian Johnson, *The Souls of China: The Return of Religion After Mao*

Stephen Alford, *London's Triumph: Merchant Adventurers and the Tudor City*

Hugo Mercier and Dan Sperber, *The Enigma of Reason: A New Theory of Human Understanding*

Stuart Hall, *Familiar Stranger: A Life Between Two Islands*

Allen Ginsberg, *The Best Minds of My Generation: A Literary History of the Beats*

Sayeeda Warsi, *The Enemy Within: A Tale of Muslim Britain*

Alexander Betts and Paul Collier, *Refuge: Transforming a Broken Refugee System*

Robert Bickers, *Out of China: How the Chinese Ended the Era of Western Domination*

Erica Benner, *Be Like the Fox: Machiavelli's Lifelong Quest for Freedom*

William D. Cohan, *Why Wall Street Matters*

David Horspool, *Oliver Cromwell: The Protector*

Daniel C. Dennett, *From Bacteria to Bach and Back: The Evolution of Minds*

Derek Thompson, *Hit Makers: How Things Become Popular*

Harriet Harman, *A Woman's Work*

Wendell Berry, *The World-Ending Fire: The Essential Wendell Berry*

Daniel Levin, *Nothing but a Circus: Misadventures among the Powerful*

Stephen Church, *Henry III: A Simple and God-Fearing King*

Pankaj Mishra, *Age of Anger: A History of the Present*

Graeme Wood, *The Way of the Strangers: Encounters with the Islamic State*

Michael Lewis, *The Undoing Project: A Friendship that Changed the World*

John Romer, *A History of Ancient Egypt, Volume 2: From the Great Pyramid to the Fall of the Middle Kingdom*

Andy King, *Edward I: A New King Arthur?*

Thomas L. Friedman, *Thank You for Being Late: An Optimist's Guide to Thriving in the Age of Accelerations*

John Edwards, *Mary I: The Daughter of Time*

Grayson Perry, *The Descent of Man*

Deyan Sudjic, *The Language of Cities*

Norman Ohler, *Blitzed: Drugs in Nazi Germany*

Carlo Rovelli, *Reality Is Not What It Seems: The Journey to Quantum Gravity*

Catherine Merridale, *Lenin on the Train*

Susan Greenfield, *A Day in the Life of the Brain: The Neuroscience of Consciousness from Dawn Till Dusk*

Christopher Given-Wilson, *Edward II: The Terrors of Kingship*

Emma Jane Kirby, *The Optician of Lampedusa*

Minoo Dinshaw, *Outlandish Knight: The Byzantine Life of Steven Runciman*

Candice Millard, *Hero of the Empire: The Making of Winston Churchill*

Christopher de Hamel, *Meetings with Remarkable Manuscripts*

Brian Cox and Jeff Forshaw, *Universal: A Guide to the Cosmos*

Ryan Avent, *The Wealth of Humans: Work and Its Absence in the Twenty-first Century*

Jodie Archer and Matthew L. Jockers, *The Bestseller Code*

Cathy O'Neil, *Weapons of Math Destruction: How Big Data Increases Inequality and Threatens Democracy*

Peter Wadhams, *A Farewell to Ice: A Report from the Arctic*

Richard J. Evans, *The Pursuit of Power: Europe, 1815-1914*

Anthony Gottlieb, *The Dream of Enlightenment: The Rise of Modern Philosophy*

Brendan Simms, *Britain's Europe: A Thousand Years of Conflict and Cooperation*

Slavoj Žižek, *Against the Double Blackmail: Refugees, Terror, and Other Troubles with the Neighbours*

Lynsey Hanley, *Respectable: The Experience of Class*

Piers Brendon, *Edward VIII: The Uncrowned King*

Matthew Desmond, *Evicted: Poverty and Profit in the American City*

T.M. Devine, *Independence or Union: Scotland's Past and Scotland's Present*

Seamus Murphy, *The Republic*

Jerry Brotton, *This Orient Isle: Elizabethan England and the Islamic World*

Srinath Raghavan, *India's War: The Making of Modern South Asia, 1939-1945*

Clare Jackson, *Charles II: The Star King*

Nandan Nilekani and Viral Shah, *Rebooting India: Realizing a Billion Aspirations*

Sunil Khilnani, *Incarnations: India in 50 Lives*

Helen Pearson, *The Life Project: The Extraordinary Story of Our Ordinary Lives*

Ben Ratliff, *Every Song Ever: Twenty Ways to Listen to Music Now*

Richard Davenport-Hines, *Edward VII: The Cosmopolitan King*

Peter H. Wilson, *The Holy Roman Empire: A Thousand Years of Europe's History*

Todd Rose, *The End of Average: How to Succeed in a World that Values Sameness*

Frank Trentmann, *Empire of Things: How We Became a World of Consumers, from the Fifteenth Century to the Twenty-First*

Laura Ashe, *Richard II: A Brittle Glory*

John Donvan and Caren Zucker, *In a Different Key: The Story of Autism*

Jack Shenker, *The Egyptians: A Radical Story*

Tim Judah, *In Wartime: Stories from Ukraine*

Serhii Plokhy, *The Gates of Europe: A History of Ukraine*

Robin Lane Fox, *Augustine: Conversions and Confessions*

Peter Hennessy and James Jinks, *The Silent Deep: The Royal Navy Submarine Service Since 1945*

Sean McMeekin, *The Ottoman Endgame: War, Revolution and the Making of the Modern Middle East, 1908–1923*

Charles Moore, *Margaret Thatcher: The Authorized Biography, Volume Two: Everything She Wants*

Dominic Sandbrook, *The Great British Dream Factory: The Strange History of Our National Imagination*

Larissa MacFarquhar, *Strangers Drowning: Voyages to the Brink of Moral Extremity*

Niall Ferguson, *Kissinger: 1923-1968: The Idealist*

Carlo Rovelli, *Seven Brief Lessons on Physics*

Tim Blanning, *Frederick the Great: King of Prussia*

Ian Kershaw, *To Hell and Back: Europe, 1914–1949*

Pedro Domingos, *The Master Algorithm: How the Quest for the Ultimate Learning Machine Will Remake Our World*

David Wootton, *The Invention of Science: A New History of the Scientific Revolution*